Rural Britain Then & Now

Rural Britain Then & Now

Roger Hunt

Foreword by Sir Simon Jenkins

CASSELL ILLUSTRATED

For my parents

First published in Great Britain in 2004 by Cassell Illustrated,
a division of Octopus Publishing Group Limited
2–4 Heron Quays, London E14 4JP

A CIP catalogue record for this book is
available from the British Library.

ISBN 1 84403 043 1

ADDITIONAL RESEARCH BY Belinda Bamber
DESIGN BY Ken Wilson
JACKET DESIGN AND ART DIRECTION BY Jo Knowles
PUBLISHING MANAGER Anna Cheifetz

Printed in China

Contents

A Note on Francis Frith

Francis Frith, and those that continued his work, recorded the development of Britain over a period of more than one hundred years. Their photographic legacy represents a truly remarkable insight into the changing face of the countryside and its people.

Francis Frith

Born in Chesterfield in 1822 to Quaker parents, Frith was sent away to boarding school at the age of twelve, four years later becoming apprenticed to a cutler in Sheffield. He appears to have suffered some kind of nervous breakdown before going on to establish a successful grocery business in Liverpool. This financed the opening of a small printing company which, when he sold in 1856, had a turnover of £200,000 a year.

Frith was attracted by the new art of photography and was already a respected amateur when, between 1856 and 1859, he undertook photographic expeditions up the Nile and in the Holy Land that involved not only the use of enormously cumbersome equipment – including fragile glass photographic plates, chemicals and a darkroom – but also great personal danger.

With his fame and reputation as a photographer now established, he married Mary Anne Rosling in 1859 and settled in her family's home town of Reigate, Surrey. Here he set up the photographic firm, Francis Frith and Co.

It was in 1860 that he began the work that was to consume him for the rest of his life. He set out to record a photographic image of every city, town and village in Britain also capturing churches, rivers, great houses, mills and landscapes. In this task he was assisted by photographic assistants and later by his children. The images were sold in their millions as souvenir photographs and later as picture postcards.

Frith died in Cannes, France, in 1898. The company was taken over by his children and grandchildren, but it finally ceased trading in 1971. Today the archive is marketed as The Francis Frith Collection based in Teffont, Salisbury, Wiltshire and through the internet Frith's photographs are now more accessible than ever before – see *www.francisfrith.co.uk*.

Foreword by Sir Simon Jenkins

Rural Britain is a novel concept. Once upon a time the essence of any nation was rurality. Britain was a sea of hills, fields and trees in which settlements were islands. The countryside was populated, but in cottages and villages that owed their existence to the landscape. Britain lived off the countryside and depended on the countryside.

Until recently those recording the state of Britain wandered through an unchanging scenery of images such as those in this book. From Celia Fiennes and Jonathan Swift to William Cobbett and George Borrow, they witnessed country people and country institutions. Between the world wars, travellers such as H.V. Morton and Arthur Mee treated national culture as rural, and urbanism as an aberration. Morton avoided towns when he went 'in search of England'. He knew when he reached the edge of the city, at a tollgate, inn or last row of houses. Come the first hedgerow and 'the keen air was like wine to me, the green of the young leaves was like music'.

Today Morton and others would be shocked. Rural Britain is suffering terrible abuse. The controls introduced to counter the ribbon development of the 1930s are in decay. For half a century development has been contained within or round existing settlement. The movement to save old buildings, begun by William Morris in the nineteenth century, increased awareness of country architecture. It protected churches, farms and manors. A sort of line was held.

By the end of the twentieth century the pressure for building seemed irresistible. Outside national parks and specifically protected areas, countryside is no longer safe. Town centres have been allowed to empty and colonise their surrounding counties. Fields and woods across southern England are sprouting housing and industrial estates, hypermarkets, warehouses, pylons, masts and wind turbines. The occupation of rural Britain is running at the rate of a city the size of Bristol every five years.

This has been fuelled by a change in the rural economy. Many of the country people depicted in these photographs could not live in the same villages today. Their crafts have died and their children moved to the city. Farming is being replaced by 'ex-urban' activities, by commuting, sport and leisure, by second homes and retirement cottages. Only a small minority of those living in villages work on the land. But while the residents, and the economy, of rural Britain may have changed, the visual impact of what survives is remarkably constant. It is still green. It is still beautiful.

The social condition of rural Britain bears no comparison with the picturesque poverty of a century ago. But as a backdrop for what we now value in the country I find it as vivid as ever. We can note the change in road surfaces, vehicles, clothes and cleanliness. But the church and the inn, the shop and the cottage, the farm and the village street are there still. The countryside remains cherished and valued by those who occupy it. New people may love it in new ways and for new reasons. But love it they do, and want to see it guarded. This book shows us what we must fight to protect.

Sir Simon Jenkins

Part One **The Rural Setting**

Britain was born out of the countryside; from hills and fields, streams and mountains, moors and downs, fens and forests: places where nature's architecture and man's industry have, over millennia, combined. It is where many people living in a town or city today have their roots, for, although urbanising rapidly, the nation was still essentially rural when Alexandrina Victoria became Queen Victoria in the early hours of 20 June 1837.

She was just eighteen years of age and her reign was to last until her death in 1901. Importantly, those sixty-four years represent a period during which the population more than doubled and included the first generation to be photographed.

Much of the physical structure and visual appearance of the contemporary rural landscape was already present at Victoria's accession. The hierarchical structure of rural society – landlord, tenant farmer and labourer – was present too. For generations, people had lived in cottages along the village street or in isolated farmhouses, scattered hamlets or woodland huts. They were largely self-sufficient in producing their own food and essentials for living, for the most part, functioning effectively as communities.

Passing through a village, the visitor would detect an air of purpose amongst the men and women going about their chores, the tenant farmers and agricultural workers in the fields and the craftsmen in their workshops. All were imbued with a strong local culture, and a dialect to match. To a great extent they were the guardians of Britain's countryside; the landscape and buildings they inhabited generally formed a pastoral whole, little changed for a century or more. To most country people this was their workplace and home, embracing their life and ambitions.

The scene was, in the main, one of beauty, tranquillity and visual diversity; and, on the surface at least, peace. This was the rural Britain that Francis Frith sought to record when he set out with his photographic equipment in the 1860s.

However, the countryside, like the towns and cities, had for several decades been undergoing radical transformation, driven by changes in agriculture and by the revolution in technology, trade and transportation. There was frequently desperate poverty, which worsened during the agricultural depression of the 1870s, with many villagers leaving to find work in the towns or to set sail for North America or the Antipodes. Much of the poverty was a consequence of the unprecedented rise in Britain's population – from fifteen to thirty-five million over the course of Victoria's reign – which overwhelmed the traditional economic and governmental mechanisms for coping with it.

The proportion of the population employed in agriculture, twenty per cent of the total in 1901, has since declined to less than one per cent. Today, out of a population of fifty-nine million, only 375,000 are employed in the farming industry. However, just as old songs are adapted over the generations, the story – about people, place and tradition – continues. The fact that we so value highly the rural legacy handed down to us by our forebears says much for the quality of their custodianship.

Britain before Frith

While geology and climate are largely responsible for the underlying physical appearance of Britain's landscape, much of what we see today is the product of changes introduced by man. Initially, these were to make possible his physical survival; with time they developed into a need to create a sustainable and economically viable society which, until the Industrial Revolution, was largely based on agriculture.

Around 8,000 years ago, following a rapid warming in the climate and a rise in the sea level, the English Channel was formed, cutting Britain off from Continental Europe. At that time, most of the landscape was densely covered in woodland and small groups of hunter-gatherers roamed the landscape, living off whatever they could find.

Agriculture probably arrived in Britain with new settlers to the island around 4000 BC. Their most important crops were wheat and barley and, at harvest time, they stored any surplus in pits sealed with clay so that it was available in times of need. The main livestock animals were sheep, goats, cattle and pigs.

PREVIOUS PAGES: Buttermere in the Lake District with High Stile rising above, 1889. While farming in remote areas such as the Lakes has changed little in the century since this image was taken, the landscape itself now generates income from the visitors that come to enjoy it.

BELOW: Hambledon Hill, Dorset. It may appear to be an unspoilt landscape but the sinuous curves of this Iron Age hill fort, built over 2,500 years ago, are a clear example of how man has been modifying and exploiting the countryside for centuries.

RIGHT: Religious and spiritual activities as well as the growth of communities have altered the landscape since the earliest times. The ancient stone circle on Salisbury Plain is now an internationally recognised World Heritage Site and has been dated back to around 2000 BC, but it is still shrouded in mystery.

Rural Britain

BELOW: Avebury, the Cove, Wiltshire, 1899. Land use has altered over thousands of years. The great stone circle encompassing part of the village of Avebury is enclosed by a ditch and external bank. The twin megaliths known as the Cove stand near the centre but seem to have been virtually disregarded when these buildings were erected.

RIGHT: Roman ruins, Wroxeter, Shropshire, c 1864. In a few areas, the modern trend of encroaching urbanisation has been reversed, and land has actually fallen back to rural use. Wroxeter was the fourth largest city in Roman Britain, but much of the area around the remaining ruins is again now used for agriculture.

The Rural Setting

Rural Britain

With the beginning of the Bronze Age, in around 2000 BC, field systems began to be laid out and land tenure to be formalised. By the beginning of the Iron Age, in about 750 BC, Britain's population was around three million. Ploughing became more efficient with the arrival of the iron plough point and two-field rotation was introduced, with crops followed by fallow in alternate years. By the time of the Roman invasion in the first century, much of the land had been cleared, with woodland cover at around eleven per cent, a proportion that remained, remarkably, more or less constant until the eighteenth century. As a result, heather moors spread out across the damp and acid uplands. In sandy lowlands scrubland and heaths were created, while the chalk areas became open grassland.

Between AD 100 and 410, the majority of Britain was part of the Roman Empire. The population grew from four to five million and, although many lived in the increasingly sophisticated and prosperous towns, most people lived in the countryside, with agriculture boosted by the development of urban markets, a money economy and efficient road-links and transport.

The early Anglo-Saxon settlements were chiefly rural and the familiar pattern of clustered village communities, manor houses and churches started to take shape. An open-field system developed, with strips allocated to community members; three-field rotation was also practised, with fields lying fallow only one year in three, which led to increased productivity. Livestock included sheep – it is estimated that by 1100 there were around three million – which were penned in small enclosures around the village. Pigs were kept in the forest where firewood was also gathered, while cattle grazed on common pastureland. The main crops were corn, wheat, oats and rye, beans and barley.

The Norman invasion of 1066, while momentous in its socio-political impact, did not physically change the settlement pattern established by the Anglo-Saxons. By 1086, the time of the Domesday Book – an inventory of the country's land, buildings and livestock – the total population was two million. Forty per cent of these people were villeins, prosperous peasants who farmed around forty acres; thirty per cent were bordars and cottars, peasants who farmed small landholdings of ten and five acres respectively, in return for service to the manorial lord. Included within this latter group were the village craftsmen.

Each village community brewed its own ale, caught deer, hares and rabbits in the woods, baked its own bread, ground its own flour and grew flax for linen. It had its own blacksmith, a carpenter to repair the ploughs and create timber-framed houses, a pounder to repair the fences, a stonemason, a beekeeper, and a steward who handled communication between lord and tenants.

By the end of the thirteenth century there had been three centuries of sustained growth. The efficient management of both farms and estates meant that it was a prosperous time for the countryside, with villagers selling their surplus produce to local towns in exchange for money. The sheep flock had expanded to twenty million animals, and wool was the country's most important industry. The proportion of the population living in towns increased to around twenty per cent, a figure which remained constant until the eighteenth century.

The urban economy expanded and international trade was buoyant. However, the rapidly growing population – around seven million at this time – increased the demand for food, requiring marginal land – including marsh, heath and woodland – to be brought under cultivation.

Around 1290 the climate became colder and less stable, with dramatic effects on agriculture. Prolonged wet weather caused a great famine between 1315 and 1322. This was followed by the Black Death of 1348 to 1350. Together, these events claimed the lives of about half the population, reducing it to between three and four million, and it was not to return to its former levels until the seventeenth century. The farming community was devastated; sheep and cattle wandered through crops, and with few tenants left to work it, cultivated land reverted to scrub. Yet, for those peasants who survived, the balance of economic power turned in their favour. They were able to negotiate contracts with landlords, giving them more favourable conditions of tenure, and the more successful created consolidated holdings, enclosing land in the process.

Woollen cloth remained the country's chief export, bringing great wealth to some areas, with vast tracts of land given over to the grazing of sheep. The rise of the yeoman in the sixteenth century, who farmed his own landholdings, as opposed to the tenant who paid rent, saw a new type of farmer and one who often became rich and could be elevated to the class of gentleman in the process.

The period from 1600 to 1750 saw considerable changes in agriculture, as subsistence farming was replaced by an efficient industry with surpluses to export. Key innovations included the introduction of the seed drill by Jethro Tull and four-crop rotation by 'Turnip' Townsend. As the rotation included a root crop, much larger numbers of animals could be overwintered, so that fresh meat became available for most of the year. Agricultural societies and shows were established to disseminate the new techniques and new crops included potatoes, cauliflower and spinach. At the same time the practice of enclosure increased drastically, so that small farmers often found themselves landless.

Between 1750 and 1850 the pace of change accelerated, both in the countryside and towns. It was accompanied by rapid population growth – from nine million in 1750 to eighteen million in 1850, by which time over half the population lived in towns. The stage was set for the changes that we explore as we chart the history of rural Britain to the present day.

Class and ownership

For much of the nineteenth century, the power wielded in the countryside by the landed class, much of it aristocratic, was virtually absolute. However, by the closing decades of Victoria's reign, change was in the air. The Reform Act of 1884 had extended the electorate to include agricultural

BELOW: Erlestoke, Wiltshire, 1900. Frith captured this village on the edge of Salisbury Plain just before the two World Wars effected the greatest changes of the twentieth century on both settlements and farming methods in rural Britain.

RIGHT: Hutton-le-Hole, North Yorkshire, today and in 1955. Some places have seen extensive and inappropriate development but here the wide greens that distinguish the village have altered little in the intervening years and the changes that have taken place have been in keeping with the overall aesthetics.

18

labourers. The Local Government Act of 1888, which created the county councils, took away from the squires the administrative role they had played for centuries and gave it to elected officials while the gentry as a whole suffered economically from the depression in agriculture. For many, the introduction of death duties in 1894 – a measure which more or less guaranteed that inherited estates would diminish – was the final straw, and they sold their land.

As many village memorials attest, the losses the gentry and aristocracy sustained in the First World War were disproportionately heavy. The decline in agricultural incomes, briefly interrupted during the war, continued in the 1920s, reaching a new low in the 1930s. There was a drastic reduction in the number of domestic servants matched by a general decline in deference; people were less ready to doff their cap and accept what they were told without question. By the end of the Second World War, the whole structure of society had changed. By 1950 the National Trust had already acquired forty-two of the larger country houses and the owners of many others needed to open their doors to visitors and look at other sources of income in order to stay solvent and maintain the fabric of the buildings.

By the 1960s and 1970s, financial institutions and pension funds were investing heavily in land, particularly in the highly productive arable areas of East Anglia and Lincolnshire. Farmland values were fuelled by Britain's entry into the European Economic Community (later the European Union) in 1973 and the grants it was making to boost food production. At the same time there were steady advances in agricultural technology. Institutional ownership of arable land reached its peak in 1984 but, at this point, the tide turned

with the first sign of a clampdown on subsidies and land was sold both to their agricultural tenants and to property developers. Some land was bought on the back of the stock market boom of the 1980s as those with money, just as had happened in earlier times, sought the prestige of a country estate.

Recent developments

It was not only the wealthy who were looking to live in the country. The shift to the cities peaked early in the twentieth century and today the trend has shifted into reverse as people seek a better quality of life in the countryside. Many see the rewards of rural living as sufficient reason to spend long hours commuting to their jobs in urban areas. For others, computer technology allows them to work from home, all or at least some of the time, with the result that they can earn good incomes while improving the quality of their work and home life. Some 2.2 million people telework and it is estimated that almost a quarter of Britons could do so. The self-employed are particularly vital to the rural economy as they spend their earnings in the local shops and get involved in community life.

Guardianship of the countryside itself remains largely the responsibility of the farming community. Subsidies are becoming rare for food production and the farming industry is increasingly divided between large-scale producers and smaller scale, high-value-added operations concentrating on niche markets. Currently, the fastest growing sector of food production is the organic market, with its emphasis on sustainable agriculture and animal welfare. In addition, the growth of interest in gourmet foods has created a luxury market in rare breeds and unusual cheeses that are the preserve of small, dedicated rural enterprises.

The changing face of agriculture has moulded the shape and look of the countryside over nearly seven millennia. In recent decades, intensive agriculture has had a negative impact on the visual and environmental quality and diversity of the landscape, while the fall in prices received by the farmer has had a similarly destructive effect on farm incomes.

The Rural Setting

Rural Britain   Diversification is, however, increasing. Many farmers are now looking to tourism and recreation. They are also reacting to the backlash against chemicals in agriculture, prompted in part by the organic food, wildlife and green lobbies. Some are adopting environmentally friendly farming practice and investigating the generation of green energy through wind-power and biofuels. Rural life goes on – it has simply come up to date to survive.

Landscape

Britain's landscape – beautiful, complex and often of astonishing variety – has evolved over millions of years. From the very earliest times the earth's forces have manifested their might, shifting and folding the surface and laying down beds of rocks, sands and soils that have been further moulded by the rain, wind and sun.

Man has also played his part, working the landscape not just for the production of food, but through mining, quarrying and harnessing the power of rivers and streams. Huge tracts of land have been transformed, often radically. The centuries-long process of reclamation of the fens of East Anglia and Lincolnshire created fertile areas. Meanwhile, in places such as the Scottish Highlands, cottagers were cleared to create huge sheep ranches some of which later become sporting estates offering grouse shooting, deerstalking and fly fishing. Many Victorian landowners planted vast woodlands; the centuries-old tradition of laying out deer-parks began to pick up pace and by 1892 there were four hundred.

All of this has resulted in a unique diversity of countryside and buildings. It has also shaped the way people think, the food they eat and the way they live their everyday lives. As a result, the regions of Britain comprise a number of fascinating and sometimes quirky entities; places where one can savour individuality not just in landscape, but through a rich variety of dialects, foods, customs, sayings, architecture and farming practices, as well as distinctive features such as hedgerows, dry stone walls and ancient trees.

LEFT, *left to right*: Britain's diverse rural landscape has always offered itself to a wide variety of uses including cereal growing, livestock, tourism, hunting and forestry. Dry stone walled fields and moors near Chitheroe, Lancashire reflect age-old farming practices; heather in bloom on Egton Moor, North Yorkshire, where the moorland is working countryside, supporting rural employment through farming and grouse shooting; Westerdale, North Yorkshire where a patchwork of fields supports both crops and livestock; and Loch Affric reflecting a mixture of plantation and ancient Caledonian Forest, near Inverness, Scotland, which is a melding of man-made and natural landscape.

BELOW: The head of Great Langdale in the heart of the Lake District. Such landscapes have evolved over millions of years as the earth's forces have shifted and folded the surface and laid down beds of rocks, sands and soils, further moulded by the rain, wind and sun.

Rural Britain

Arable crops and market gardening dominate the flatter land and richer soils of the south east. To the west and north lie areas of lush grass that are perfect for cattle and as a consequence are known for their meat and dairy products. In the more mountainous uplands of Wales, the Peak District and Scotland, sheep are the mainstay of rural communities, often cared for on small farms that have been in the same family for generations.

The evolution of the landscape is a never ending process, with villages expanding or changing and new farming practices bringing with them fresh shapes, textures and colour palettes as evidenced by the brilliant yellow of the recently introduced rape. As a consequence, there has been a shift in the pattern of flora and fauna; the latter includes some of the richest ranges of bird life in Europe.

In the rebuilding of Britain after 1945, many rural villages gained mains water, electricity and sewerage, which meant the gradual loss of small local landmarks like ponds, pumps and wells. At the same time the alien forms of pylons started stalking the landscape, telephone wires looped across village streets and television aerials sprouted from rooftops.

While the villages, particularly those within commuting distance of large towns, began to spread outwards as new houses were built, households increasingly acquired one or more cars with the result that lanes became roads accompanied by road-signs, lighting and service stations. Other settlements dwindled in size, with schools, shops and other amenities closing.

In more recent years there has been an awareness of the need to protect the countryside, make the best use of land and improve the quality and attractiveness of residential areas. Planners are being required to interpret government guidelines that call upon local authorities and developers to think imaginatively about design and townscape without compromising the environment. In so doing, they are moving closer to creating places and spaces with the needs of people in mind, which are attractive, have their own distinctive identity, and both respect and enhance local character.

This is helping to reverse the tide of uniformity that threatened to impose a universal 'vernacular' on the countryside in the mid-twentieth century. Whereas many town centres are now indistinguishable and interchangeable throughout Britain, the individuality of rural areas is being restored through the use of local materials.

Geography

Measured from its extremities, Britain is some 600 miles long and 320 miles wide, an island of often remarkable beauty with a diversity of landscapes that is probably unmatched in an area of such small size anywhere else in the world.

Scotland has Britain's highest mountain, the 4,406-foot drama of Ben Nevis, while Wales has Snowdon, which rises to 3,560 feet. The majestic starkness of the uplands is in marked contrast to the lowlands of the south east, where there is a harmony of undulating scarp lands and fertile farmlands.

BELOW: Rosendale, North York Moors, Yorkshire. Agriculture alone is not responsible for the habitation of rural areas. Many communities have developed, like this mining village, to exploit natural resources such as coal, tin and lead. The long, thin design of this 'street' village, has been influenced by the road pattern.

RIGHT: Ilkley, the moors, West Yorkshire, 1914. This peaceful scene belies the fact that in Europe the First World War was beginning. The war effected significant change in rural areas – both depopulating them and forcing change in traditional agricultural methods.

Like a spider's web thrown across the landscape, there are myriad streams, tracks and field boundaries. These have a vital interrelationship with the settlement pattern that has grown up since man first inhabited Britain.

Villages may be on hills, mountainsides or in valley bottoms, yet it is rare that they have come to occupy a particular site purely through some random whim of their builders. Most have grown up because there is an eminently practical reason for them being there; it might be that they offer a vantage point, are at a river crossing, have a spring of good water, or are close to fertile land. The Romans and Saxons generally settled in sites that had been occupied by earlier generations, a trend that has continued ever since.

In some cases villages were built by estate owners to ensure the presence of a workforce; others were moved to new locations by landowners in order to create parkland or to preserve their personal privacy. Many villages fall into two structural categories: 'street' and 'green'. The former are long and thin, strung out along a road; the latter huddle around a village green. Most have not been planned but have been adapted over time to meet the changing needs of the community.

GEOLOGY

Britain has a rich variety of stone and mineral deposits. These have contributed not only to the success of a wide variety of industries but have also led to the distinctive variations in colour, texture and style of the buildings. Many towns and villages had their own quarries, with the stone known by the quarry it came from. There was grey Barnack stone from Northamptonshire and honey-toned Chilmark from Wiltshire.

The chief building stones used in Britain are limestone, sandstone and granite. There are, however, great variations within these broad categories, depending partly on which geological stratum they come from.

Limestone can be found in four different strata: Cretaceous, Jurassic, Permian and Carboniferous. The Jurassic limestone belt sweeps from Dorset to Yorkshire. It includes the mellow, golden Cotswold stone, which has been used for building since Roman times. It can be found in major historic landmarks like Windsor Castle and Blenheim Palace, and is still quarried for cottages in the picturesque towns and villages of the Cotswolds.

Sandstone is found in an enormous number of geological systems formed between two million and 500 million years ago, mostly in the Cretaceous, Triassic and Carboniferous. It produces a wide variety of colours, thanks to the mix of particles of quartz, minerals like mica and feldspar, and fragments of shell. Its pale greys, pinks, purples and greens enhance the interior of many a parish church in the Malvern Hills, Shropshire and the Lake District.

The best building granites come from Scotland and Cornwall. Scottish granite, a dark and somewhat gloomy grey, has been used to construct many picturesque castles overlooking remote lochs; the slightly lighter coloured Cornish stone has been used for coastal cottages which withstand the full force of the sea spray.

CLOCKWISE FROM TOP: Sandstone buildings in Bainbridge, Wensleydale, Yorkshire; simple stone dressings used around a window; Cotswold limestone gives the houses at Lower Turkdean in Gloucestershire a warm and mellow appearance. Local building stones dictate architectural styles and often make it seem as if the buildings have been hewn from the landscape.

BELOW: Clovelly, Devon. Hemmed in by steep hills, stone dominates the scene giving the buildings, the tumbling cobbled streets and the harbour wall a solidity that is both aesthetic and real.

LEFT AND MAIN PICTURE:
Harlech Castle, Gwynedd, Wales, today and in 1889. Built between 1283 and 1289 for King Edward I, it is now a World Heritage Site. Castles were constructed both for defence and to act as a dominant and ever-present symbol and reminder of the monarch's power over the land.

The homes of the poor

Until the sixteenth century, cottages – the houses of cottars and labourers – were invariably one- or two-room hovels. The walls were made of wattle and daub, hazel rods covered with clay; in the south west they were formed of cob: mud mixed with lime. The floors were of beaten earth or sometime chalk and they were roofed with reed, straw or turf. The windows were formed of simple open grilles of wood or reed, and some had wooden shutters. The construction of such buildings was flimsy and they were often rebuilt or repaired by each generation, so little remains today of such structures.

Many of the cottages which do survive date from the period known as the Great Rebuilding, a phase of new and more robust building that lasted from the late sixteenth to the early eighteenth century, and represents the culmination of the vernacular style. By the nineteenth century, however, the stock of vernacular cottages was in decline, and many farm workers lived in damp and squalid conditions. Enlightened landlords were willing to improve dilapidated buildings, although they were less likely to use local materials. The prosperous period of the 1850s and 1860s saw an upsurge in 'model' estate cottages.

In the 1890s the cottages that were built reflected legislation to improve sanitation, ventilation and light; their designs were simple and effective, although somewhat characterless. These included the first council houses, built in order to provide housing at affordable rents. To those living in dilapidated, damp and cold cottages with no plumbing, they were very appealing.

Few of the earlier rural buildings knew an architect, with most evolving over time, adapted to suit the fashions and needs of the period and those owning them. There are many tell-tale signs of change; windows may be unaligned or in odd positions, or of different styles and patterns. Frequently, it is clear that the roofline has changed, as has the detailing of the brick and stone courses and other embellishment.

Roof coverings have frequently been altered over the years. Many buildings were originally thatched, some were later

LEFT: Calmsden, Gloucestershire. Estate cottages were built by enlightened landlords to improve the lot of their workers, who had previously lived in damp and cold, if not squalid conditions. Many are now seen as desirable holiday homes.

BELOW: St Mary's Scilly Isles, Cornwall, 1892. The granite of which the Scilly Isles comprise was used to build the village's cottages, but because the stones were often of differing sizes they were not always laid in regular courses. The year before this photograph was taken the census recorded that the population of the 1,554-acre St Mary's was 1,201 persons.

GARDENS

The rural scene would not be what it is without its gardens. Large and small, they frequently burst with a profusion of pastel shades to conjure romance, nostalgia and beauty and, when coupled with superb examples of vernacular architecture, are irresistible.

In medieval times, walled gardens in monasteries were used for growing herbs for both culinary and medicinal purposes. Garden design, as we currently understand it, began in the sixteenth century, influenced by Italian, French a nd Dutch ideas. This was, however, only for the gardens of the gentry and aristocracy.

For the humble and impoverished cottager, the contemplation of beauty was secondary to the need to feed the family, so the growing of flowers took second place to the cultivation of vegetables, fruit and herbs. Allotments, still a familiar sight today, became increasingly popular in Victorian times, since they allowed extra space for growing produce.

Most agricultural workers worked long hours, so it was often a case of digging by the light of the 'parish lantern', the moon. However, for some cottagers there was a competitive edge to their toil as they fought for first prize in the increasingly popular vegetable, fruit and flower shows.

Many cottage plants now considered traditionally British, such as lupins, Michaelmas daisies, chrysanthemum and sweet peas, were introduced from abroad, first from western Europe and later from America, Africa and Asia. The Victorians did much experimenting, particularly with roses, creating many hybrid varieties.

The effect on the landscape of creating areas for pleasure was, in some places, considerable; the parkland of some of the larger houses extended over several parishes, with thousands of trees planted. Many trees imported from North America were introduced into nineteenth-century arboreta, including the Douglas fir, the Sitka spruce and Lawson's cypress, while rhododendrons also took hold in woods and parks.

Our present obsession with gardening is comparatively recent. Before the late 1950s, only nurseries sold plants and, rather than being pot-grown, the majority were lifted straight from the ground and then sold and planted in the dormant season. Today, the interest in garden design is huge and owners of even quite small gardens will pay for advice on how to transform their modest patch.

ABOVE LEFT: Court Cottage, Cockington, Devon, 1889. Our present obsession with gardening is comparatively recent. For the humble and impoverished cottager, the contemplation of beauty was less important than the need to feed the family, so the growing of flowers took second place to the cultivation of vegetables, fruit and herbs.

BELOW LEFT: Eastnor, Herefordshire. Many cottage plants now considered traditionally British were introduced from abroad, first from Western Europe and later from America, Africa and Asia. They added intensity of colour, but at the expense of many wild flowers.

RIGHT: Grove Place, Padstow, Cornwall, 1920. Many cottages were not designed with gardening for leisure in mind. Fruit and vegetables were often grown in allotments and small, easily tended gardens provided a relief from the cramped surroundings in which some rural people lived.

Rural Britain tiled and, in the nineteenth century, Welsh slate, which is light and easily split, was often employed.

The cycle of replacing local materials with cheaper products from elsewhere has come full circle: conservation officers now ask for old houses to be repaired using local bricks, tiles and stone.

Today, cottage homes are highly desirable and generally command large sums when they come onto the market. In the building of new homes, the planners of recent years are much concerned with maintaining the vernacular style and developers are less likely to be permitted to build the 'boxes' of the recent past when undertaking new schemes. One of the more difficult areas is the reuse of farm buildings. Barns in particular offer many attractions when converted into homes, although they present problems to those seeking to maintain the sense of space, atmosphere and history that made them special in the first place.

Materials and regional styles

Before the advent of canals and railways, which allowed building materials to be readily transported, people exploited what they could find in the surrounding landscape; as a result, a rich diversity of vernacular building styles developed across Britain, creating distinctive regional variations.

Most adaptable of the materials was timber. The majority of houses were built using frame construction, whereby loads are carried through the frame rather than through the walls. Timber was cheap and plentiful in many parts of Britain, with a wide range of hardwoods available (although oak was most commonly used) and the local carpenter would create the building's frame using great timbers jointed and pegged together.

Across the country a variety of different timber-framing methods were utilized. With its distinctive triangular appearance, one of the most basic forms of timber framing is the cruck, where the roof load is taken through pairs of 'A' frames made from naturally-curving tree trunks. This is mostly found in the west, north and Midlands, particularly in Herefordshire. The earliest surviving buildings using this method date back to at least the thirteenth century, although it is thought that it originated much earlier. Cruck frames began to disappear in the sixteenth and seventeenth centuries with the increased demand for two-storey houses and the perfection of box-frame methods of construction.

The more complex box-frame consists of posts, which form part of the walls, linked by tie beams. A notable example is the Wealden house, which has a central hall open to the roof, flanked by two-storey bays with the upper storeys

RIGHT AND BELOW: Timber — especially oak — was once cheap and plentiful in Britain, so vast numbers of cottages and houses were built using frame construction. Local carpenters jointed and pegged together the great timbers to form a structural skeleton. Today the legacy of their craftsmanship is revealed in some of Britain's most beautiful buildings.

BELOW: Lavenham, Suffolk. The most notable features of any vernacular building include its colour and texture. Often this results from coatings of limewash, pigmented with vibrant hues. This was often applied by agricultural workers during quiet periods or when they were unable to work on the land.

RIGHT: Leatherhead, Surrey, 1906. Like many industrial buildings, the old mill was clad in weather-boarding. At one time elm was the usual choice for the boards but by the twentieth century soft-wood was being used which necessitated the application of a coat of paint or preservative.

BELOW RIGHT: Hill House Farm, Herefordshire. By the end of the eighteenth century bricks were widely used. The coming of first the canals and then the railways meant that they could be easily transported to non-clay bearing regions. As a result distinctive vernacular building styles began to disappear.

Rural Britain

'jettied' so that they projected over the ground floor structure. Kent and Sussex are dotted with such houses built by yeomen farmers to symbolise their wealth and status. In the West Midlands, Lancashire and Cheshire, it is common to find exposed timbers blackened to give the buildings a characteristic 'black and white' appearance.

The gaps between the vertical and horizontal timbers were infilled with a variety of materials, including stone and brick, often arranged in a chevron or herring-bone pattern. Although plaster and a protective coating of limewash were frequently applied over both panels and beams, nineteenth- and twentieth-century romantics treasured the look of traditional half-timbered cottages; as a consequence, many

were stripped of their plaster skins in order to expose timbers that were never intended to be seen. Fashion led to many timber-framed buildings being re-faced with brick. Others were hidden behind weather-boards and tiles, both of which were introduced in south-eastern England towards the end of the eighteenth century. Weather-boarding was common on many cottages, barns and mills and, while it originally consisted of elm boards, by the twentieth century softwood was being employed, which necessitated the application of a coat of paint or preservative.

Stone of a wide range of colours and qualities was employed, although the cost of working and transporting it meant that until the end of the medieval period, its use was largely

restricted to ecclesiastical buildings and the houses of the wealthy. Limestone and sandstone formed the walls and sometimes the roofs of a range of structures. Granite, marble, flint, pebbles, cobbles, slate and even chalk were used for walling. For the builder, each material offered different characteristics; some were easily cut and shaped, while others were remarkably resistant to weathering and were harder to work.

Stone offers an enduring diversity of colour, texture and type, from the golden hues of Cotswold limestone to the rugged grey-black of Cornish granite. There is a similarly attractive spectrum of hues in building stone quarried in the Midlands and in Wales. Travel north and sandstone in particular is the dominant material. For centuries the sandstone of Hadrian's Wall was plundered for use in the walls of farms and incorporated in fortified homesteads in Northumberland known as peel towers.

Flint was first used by the Romans and is employed in all the chalk-rich eastern and south-eastern counties. From the thirteenth century squared flints were used to create the decorative 'flush work' common in rural churches in East Anglia.

Bricks were first introduced into Britain by the Romans and the skills required to manufacture them were revived in the Middle Ages. The Tudors perfected the art of brick making, so that bricks became a prestigious alternative to stone. By the end of the eighteenth century, they were used for humble cottages.

The brick and tile maker's art adds colour, texture and simple character to buildings and is particularly evident in the south east, where the rich earth hues of the bricks and tiles give

LEFT: Aldeburgh, Suffolk. The sparkling sunlight of coastal areas has encouraged the use of succulent, 'ice cream' colours not found in rural buildings further inland.

BELOW: Swinsty Hall, West Yorkshire. Stone forms the roof, walls, window mullions and garden wall of this fifteenth century building. It was no doubt hewn from a local quarry and the quality of its dressing directly reflects the importance of the house.

Rural Britain   warmth to the buildings of the Wealden landscapes of Kent, Sussex and Surrey. In contrast, the Gault clay of Cambridgeshire produces a typically pale yellow brick that is suitably monochromatic next to the stark black fields and broad horizons of the Fenlands.

Early clay 'peg tiles' had one or two holes to accommodate wooden pegs which hooked onto laths of oak or elm. Since they were hand-made, and the firing processes were inconsistent, they have many different shapes, shades and finishes and as a result have created roofscapes of great softness.

With an 'S' shaped double curve that allows each tile to fit into the next, pantiles were brought to Britain from Holland and Belgium. They give a distinctive, southern European character to the areas where they are used, which include the eastern counties north of London up to the Scottish border and, to the west, Bridgwater in Somerset.

Quarried in Devon, Cornwall and Wales, slate has been used since the twelfth century. Its use increased dramatically during the eighteenth and nineteenth century, as first the canals and later the railways enabled it to be distributed all over the country; indeed in some areas it came close to entirely replacing thatch.

Unbaked earth, often mixed with straw, is an ancient material. Employed to construct the walls of buildings, its use was widespread in Britain until the nineteenth century. Those who live in such buildings find the thick, solid walls keep them cool in summer and snug and warm in winter. The greatest concentrations of earth-built structures are in the south west,

BELOW: St Mary and St David Church, Kilpeck, Herefordshire. The carvings in the old red sandstone around the south door date from the mid twelfth century. The cost of transporting and working stone at this time meant that its use was often limited to ecclesiastical and defensive buildings. Church building brought fine craftsmanship and European stylistic influences to rural areas in Britain.

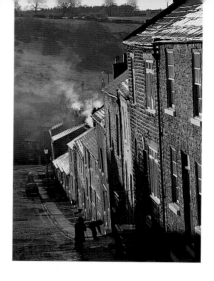

East Anglia and in parts of the Midlands. The technique is variously known as cob, clay-lump, clay-bat and Pisé.

Many buildings constructed using this material have tell-tale soft, rounded edges and gentle undulations. There is an old Devon saying that 'all cob wants is a good hat and a good pair of shoes': to prevent the penetration of water, the walls stand on a plinth of stone, flint or brick, and usually have a roof of thatch with wide overhanging eaves to throw the water clear of the walls.

Whatever the materials used to construct it, the most notable features of any vernacular building include its colour and texture. Quite often this can be as a result of coatings of limewash, pigmented with vibrant hues. Certain colours have become typical of some areas. In Suffolk, for example, shades of pink have long been popular while the range of colours in the south of the country includes blue and green as well as yellows, reds and creams; in the north and Scotland, cottages are typically whitewashed.

The Rural Setting

BELOW: Picking snowdrops c 1930. More than any other, spring is the season awaited with anticipation since the countryside is again in its first flush of youth. The early blooms signal the start of another farming year.

The rural year

The seasons – spring, summer, autumn, winter – are a powerful force in the rural life of Britain; they also bring great beauty to the countryside, changing its appearance, sometimes subtly but often dramatically. With their livelihoods frequently dependent on the effects of the natural world and the weather, country people were, and in some cases still are, very much in tune with nature. As a consequence the passing of the seasons is a major aspect of rural life and key points in the farming calendar were marked, and are still celebrated, in towns and villages all over the country.

Most of the festivities are clearly pre-Christian in origin, commemorating the important days of the Celtic year, such as the summer and winter solstices and the spring and autumn equinoxes. Most of them were, however, given a Christian meaning in the early Middle Ages in order to confer a degree of religious respectability.

Close to the beginning of the year, Candlemas Day, on 2nd February, marks the mid-point of winter, half-way between the winter solstice and the spring equinox. So named because it was the day on which the year's supply of candles for the church was blessed, it also commemorates the ritual purification of Mary 40 days after the birth of Christ. While it was observed as such as early as the 4th century AD, its pre-Christian origin is plain: it coincides with Februa, the Roman feast of purification, and with the Celtic Imbolc.

Shrove Tuesday or 'pancake day' signals the beginning of Lent. The name Shrove comes from the old word 'shrive' which means to confess. On Shrove Tuesday, in the Middle Ages, people used to confess their sins so that they were forgiven before the season of Lent began. The making of pancakes provided a useful way of using up eggs and butter forbidden during the Lenten fast and pancake races form an integral part of many village traditions.

Lady Day, on 25th March, marks the spring, or vernal, equinox, the half-way point between Candlemas and Beltane (May Day). In the Christian calendar it commemorated the Feast of the Annunciation, and was chosen because it

preceded the birth of Christ by nine months. For the farming community, it was the first quarter-day (the others are Midsummer Day, Michaelmas Day and Christmas), the time for the payment of rent and other manorial dues.

Easter, which commemorates the Resurrection, is celebrated on the first Sunday that occurs after the first full moon on or after the spring equinox; it falls between 22nd March and 25th April. Special cakes were baked at Easter – of which representatives still exist in our hot cross buns and simnel cakes – and brightly coloured eggs were also presented to friends.

May Day is the Celtic festival of Beltane. Following Celtic chronology it was the mid-point of the year. It marked the first day of summer, and was celebrated with huge bonfires to honour the sun. Traditionally, it was the day when the cattle were turned out. Maypoles were made from young trees brought in from nearby woods and, having been decorated with paint and streamers, they were set up in the middle of the village green. Bringing the maypole into the village was the key point of the celebration and the prelude to a day of dancing and festivities that also included the crowning of the May Queen and children carrying garlands of flowers in procession. It was given no Christian dimension and in the seventeenth century it was common for young men and women to spend the previous night in the woods. It is for this reason that the Puritans frowned on May Day celebrations, making maypoles illegal, briefly, in 1644.

Midsummer Day marks the summer solstice, with the longest day of the year falling around the 21st June. It was adopted by Christians as the Feast of St John the Baptist, in the way that Yule, the winter solstice, became Christmas. Bonfires used to be lit on Midsummer Eve and young people would leap through the flames for luck, while girls wove garlands of St John's Wort, a herb still used in remedies today, and practised charms to try and find out who was to be their future husband. There is still a summer solstice celebration at Stonehenge, the ancient stone circle on Salisbury Plain in Wiltshire, when white-robed Druids gather to watch the sun rising exactly over the Heel Stone.

41

Rural Britain Lammas Day, on 1st August, is a religious feast day celebrating St Peter's deliverance from prison and is a quarter day in Scotland. The name is derived from 'Loaf-mass', when a loaf made from the first ripe corn was offered in the service of Holy Communion. Until the late nineteenth century, rush-bearing continued in many villages. This involved strewing plaited rushes in the aisles of churches, a practice stemming from the time when churches lacked proper flooring.

The harvest festival, which coincides with the autumn equinox, is usually held on or around 23rd September. Traditionally, it was the biggest occasion for eating and drinking in the rural calendar, celebrating the completion of the huge communal task of gathering in the harvest. With the majority of his workers badly paid, it provided an opportunity for the farmer to demonstrate his largesse by providing ample supplies of beer and food. Following this there would be sports and games as well as singing and dancing. Today, harvest festival is celebrated by decorating churches with baskets of fruit and a variety of foods; these are subsequently distributed among the elderly.

Michaelmas Day, on 29th September, is the feast of St Michael the Archangel. It marks the end of the farming year. Traditionally, it was the time when houses and land changed hands, and farm workers and domestic servants were hired for the coming year. Goose fairs and sheep sales were held on this day for hundreds of years, and in various parts of the country Michaelmas Day continues to be known as Goose Day.

On 31st October Samhain, the Celtic New Year, is celebrated with Halloween (a contraction of 'All Hallows Eve'). It precedes All Saints Day, the commemoration of saints and martyrs, on 1st November. In the north of England the tradition of lighting bonfires became central to the Halloween celebration. In some parts of Britain Halloween was a night for mischief making and pranks, and known as Mischief Night. The Reformation, which dispensed with saints days, did away with Halloween for many Europeans, and a number of the traditions of Halloween were absorbed by Guy Fawkes' Night.

42

LEFT: Signs of summer. Despite intensive farming, crimson-headed poppies still find their way into grassy fields in East Sussex, *far left*. In Dorset, *left*, the late summer activity of harvesting gets under way as it has always done; while advances in technology have changed agricultural procedures, the rural year is still tied to the seasons.

BELOW: Parkmill, West Glamorgan, 1893. Children take a break from school (the building on the left of the picture) on a sunny day. During summer months school attendance in rural areas was often low as children helped their parents bring in the harvest.

PREVIOUS PAGES: Dorking, Surrey, Chart Lane, c 1900. Snow creates a magical rural scene. Before the age of motoring, there was less imperative or ability to clear roads.

BELOW: Holly gatherers, 1910. An attribute of winter festivals since pagan times, holly was incorporated into English Christian traditions during the medieval period. With the revival of these traditions in the nineteenth century it again became a quintessential symbol of the festive season.

Guy Fawkes' Night is celebrated on or around 5th November in commemoration of the attempt to blow up Parliament on 5th November 1605. The first bonfire was lit on the night following the discovery and foiling of the plot, when Londoners joyfully lit fires in gratitude for their king being safe. The ritual soon spread, first to Bristol in 1607, and from that time until 1859 it was a national day of thanksgiving.

Many villages still have a committee to oversee the celebrations. In the preceding weeks a huge mound of wood and other combustible material is constructed in a field or on the village green. On the night itself a guy, carefully made of sticks and straw and dressed in old clothes, is placed on top. In some places villagers form a procession, carrying burning torches to the bonfire site before hurling them onto the mound to start the blaze, signalling the commencement of a display of fireworks.

The last major festival of the year is Christmas. Christmas coincides with Yule, the winter solstice. It was not until AD 320 that the Catholic Fathers in Rome decided to make 25 December Christ's birthday, in an effort to co-opt the Yule celebrations of the Celts and Saxons. In 567 the twelve days from December 25 to Epiphany were proclaimed a sacred, festive season. Christmas, in the Middle Ages, was not a single day, but rather a period of twelve days, from December 25 to January 6. In England this lasted until the middle of the seventeenth century, when the Puritan government issued official policies outlawing all religious festivals.

Christmas remained moribund until the marriage of Victoria to Prince Albert in 1840. In Germany, many of the Christmas traditions had survived, and he brought them with him. Christmas soon became a special occasion for the Royal Family; their celebration of it emphasized the importance of family closeness and an appreciation of children, and revived the idea of the holiday meal and holiday decorations. In 1841 Prince Albert introduced the first Christmas tree to Windsor Castle.

Boxing Day, December 26th, earned its name from the boxes containing gifts of money that domestic servants received from their employers. It is also known as St Stephen's Day.

Plough Monday, the first Monday after Twelfth Night, marked the resumption of work after the Christmas holiday. Farm labourers dragged a plough dressed in ribbons and other decorations from house to house, collecting money and gifts. Before the Reformation this was for the 'ploughlights' which the men kept burning before certain images in the church to obtain a blessing for their work. In later times, it was spent on celebration in the local public house. In some areas the labourers were accompanied by sword or morris dancers, and sometimes by mummers acting the characters of the 'Corn Spirit' and 'Hopper Joe', who acted out the sowing of seed. These traditions, like many others, appeared to go into terminal decline during the late nineteenth century, but have been revived in recent decades.

The Rural Setting

Part Two **The Heart of the Countryside**

Rural Britain

While farmhouses and cottages dot the landscape and hamlets straggle alongside lanes, the heart of almost any rural community is the village. Although tangible, the essence of the village is hard to define and regional variations contribute charm and ambiguity. Derived from the Latin *villaticus*, meaning an assemblage of dwellings outside, or pertaining to, a villa, the village is an institution that long predates the Domesday Book.

In our mind, the village will have a church or chapel, pub, shop and post office, as well as a memorial to the dead of two world wars. The sound of children might emanate from a school playground and there may be a medieval manor house or a later, but rather grander, 'big house'. Some private houses will carry inscriptions or other evidence attesting to their former existence as parsonage, lock-up or almshouse. Often, they will be clustered around a green or square, where sometimes there may stand a weathered market cross or battered water pump; there may even be a tranquil pond or bubbling stream.

Such would be the perfect image for a movie director seeking quintessential Britishness – a setting where Agatha Christie's Miss Marple might step from behind a neat rose-framed cottage door. However, as in the best tradition of detective fiction, what is on the surface often belies a more complex reality.

The picturesque countenance veils a conflict between nostalgia for old ways and the inevitable drive towards improvement and innovation. This is nothing new: without change, the village as an institution could not have survived. The most striking differences between the rural Britain of the nineteenth century and that of today is the ability of the present population to venture beyond the confines of village life and gain a wider view.

Since the Industrial Revolution, there has been a consider-able ebb and flow in the rural population. In recent years, the framework of private houses, communal buildings and lanes that constitutes the village has seen an influx of urban new-comers. As a consequence, property prices have invariably been pushed up, making it difficult for locals to find affordable homes. However, the incomers spend their money at the village shop or pub and pray in the church and in so doing keep such institutions alive. The heart of the countryside does, after all, have to beat, and with farming no longer the mainstay, visitors and those that can create new businesses are, in many respects, the future.

Despite the changes, the particular quality of village life remains constant. Overhead, the sun rises and sets, the light continually changing the colours and displaying the varied textures of the clustered buildings, the passage of years enriching the timber, brick and stone with a patina of age. When compared with the drabness and planned uniformity of the city and suburb, the irregular shapes of the buildings, winding, narrow lanes, peeling paintwork and crooked farm gates conjure a nostalgia and affinity with a simpler, more natural way of life.

Church and chapel

Perhaps because of our need to step into its familiar, cool sanctity, the church is still frequently the most compelling building within a village, its only rival the pub. Its steeple or tower often visible from miles around, the church is a beacon to the traveller, a glorious treasure house to the curious. It is the keeper of secrets and witness to the ephemeral lives of generations of parishioners, both rich and poor. Local children who have long since grown up and departed for careers elsewhere return to celebrate baptisms and marriages and mourn at family funerals. For them, the place resounds with memories of hymns sung at school harvest festival services and candlelit carols at Christmas, the familiar rhythms of the Anglican liturgy providing solace even to professed atheists.

Frequently representing the oldest and most historic part of the village, and broadly similar in structure, each church is in some way unique – whether solemnly virtuous in their simplicity or rich in craftsmanship while many have distinctive furnishings and monuments. All owe their

50

preservation in some degree to the generations of parishioners who have guarded them against decay and vandalism.

Inside, there may be the tomb or bronze of a crusader, sculptures and wall paintings defaced or vandalised by iconoclasts of the sixteenth and seventeenth centuries, a rood screen that somehow survived the Civil War. Outside, the graveyard records both the high mortality of Victorian children and the longevity of a local lord's family. In the weatherworn countenances of stone gargoyles may be seen the faces of former villagers and local dignitaries, caricatured by masons.

For centuries the church was the epicentre of village life. In the days before bench seating was introduced, the church was used as a community hall as well as for religious processions and services. Trading took place, dances were held, sacred plays performed and even ale brewed when feast days were celebrated. Up until two hundred years ago, the porch was a place to transact business, where public notices were posted and where children were taught to read and write.

The roots that gave life to these buildings go back millennia, with churches frequently occupying pre-Christian sites – preaching crosses, where missionaries had their stations, were erected before the first wooden churches.

The fabric of most village churches is medieval: of approximately 14,000 parish churches in England, 12,000 are pre-Reformation. There was a burst of church building in the nineteenth century, with more than 2,000 churches built in the first fourteen years of Victoria's reign, mostly in the newly urbanised areas. The architectural style that they followed, which became known as Gothic Revival, was inspired by the Decorated style of the thirteenth and fourteenth centuries. Unfortunately, architects and patrons were not above altering, removing or defacing original architectural features in order to conform to the fashion and many medieval treasures were subjected to over-enthusiastic restoration. In so doing, much was destroyed that was authentically medieval, and an overly austere atmosphere created.

Currently, there are, thankfully, many skilled conservation architects who, with the support of local parishes, repair churches in a non-invasive way, using techniques that match

those of the original mason or carpenter. Their aim is to let the additions and alterations added over the centuries speak for themselves. They follow in the tradition of William Morris, the craftsman, poet and political activist, who was so appalled by the treatment of historic churches by his contemporaries that he founded the Society for the Protection of Ancient Buildings, an organisation that still fights for the integrity of buildings. His attentions were not always welcomed: at Burford, in Oxfordshire, the vicar threw him out with the cry 'The church, sir, is mine and I shall stand on my head in it if I choose.'

While many commentators at the time remarked upon the decline in religious observance, more than half the population continued regularly to attend church or chapel. For many the Sabbath was a day when any activity apart from eating, walking or reading the 'Good Book' was frowned upon. Servants at the manor house were still expected to get lunch ready while the gentry attended morning service; as a consequence they attended evensong instead. The squire would take his place in his private pew, often surrounded by high partitions; the rest of the congregation endured long sermons from the discomfort of hard, narrow pews.

The vicar had for centuries enjoyed the protection and patronage of the local landowner and was often the younger son of one of the local landowning families. A key figure in the community, he acted not only as moral adviser, but also took on the responsibility of organising education and poor relief, roles that were subsequently taken over by local authorities. He was assisted by a curate, who often did much of the work. The curate,

LEFT AND FAR LEFT: Amberley church and castle, West Sussex, in 1906 and as it is today. The castle is now an hotel and restaurant.

BELOW: St Cuthbert's Chapel, Lindisfarne, c 1935. Some churches have attracted, and continue to draw, pilgrims and tourists to remote areas. St Cuthbert died on Inner Farne in 687 and the chapel was built in his memory.

BELOW AND BELOW RIGHT:
Tintern Abbey, South
Wales, today and in 1890.
Founded on 9 May 1131,
Tintern was only the
second Cistercian foun-
dation in Britain, and the
first in Wales. Victorian
visitors enjoyed its
romantic and picturesque
qualities.

Rural Britain

charge of several churches in different parishes so, while a Victorian cleric would walk a few yards from vicarage to church, his present-day equivalent needs a car to dash between different services, making it harder to get to know his or her flock.

Although urban congregations have dwindled over the last hundred years – according to the Church of England around one million people were attending church services on Sundays by 2001 – village services are often better attended, partly because morning service is still an important social occasion.

Church bells ring out for wedding services on many weekends, particularly in the summer, with brides in traditional long white veils maintaining the old traditions by arriving in a pony and trap.

frequently a bachelor from a humble background, lacked the family connections of the vicar, so was often found by parishioners to be more approachable.

Following the Second World War country livings often became a reward for hard-working clerics from the towns. They might initially have lacked their predecessors' knowledge of the country, but made up for it by the strength of their commitment to the village community. Country vicars are still important figures in many places and work hard, going out at all hours to visit sick and elderly people and to comfort the bereaved.

Modern clergy are drawn from all walks of life and include women as well as men. The vicar or parson is likely to sit on education and welfare committees and may organise music, drama and youth groups. However, he or she will often have

Villagers serve on the church council, operate rotas for church flowers and cleaning, support the vicar as vergers and churchwardens and enthusiastically organise fetes and jumble sales to raise money for the upkeep of the church.

Parish churches may appear to be as permanent as the landscape itself, but areas like Norfolk sometimes boast more churches than pubs, and it is impossible to keep all of them open. This does not necessarily mean that they are abandoned or demolished. The Churches Conservation Trust was set up in 1969 to care for buildings no longer needed for parish use. It now has 325, all of which are architecturally or historically important. Occasional services are held and events such as concerts, flower festivals, talks and exhibitions take place. Other redundant churches have been deconsecrated and converted into homes or communal halls.

RIGHT: Widecombe-in-the-Moor, Devon. A testament to the former prosperity of the local tin mining trade, the spire of St Pancras (the 'Cathedral of the Moors') rises above Dartmoor. Built of local granite in the fourteenth century, the church was enlarged during the fifteenth and sixteenth centuries with money from local industry.

BELOW: The military section of the cemetery in the village of Wargrave, Berkshire, records the events that have moulded the character and lives of the local community.

The Heart of the Countryside

The clergy themselves rarely live in the rambling rectories and vicarages of the past, as they are costly to heat and maintain on a modern cleric's income and also represent a very saleable asset to the church. As a result, many vicars live in purpose-built and unremarkable houses, their traditional home having been sold off.

There are numerous non-Anglican places of worship to be found in villages. Although Roman Catholicism was influential in rural England in the nineteenth century, because it was the faith of many landowning families, their churches are usually in towns or on private estates. The Methodists, Congregationalists, Baptists, Presbyterians, Quakers and Unitarians were in a minority known collectively as the 'Free Church'. Their buildings, the earliest of which date from the seventeenth century, are plainer and, as a rule, architecturally less distinguished than the Anglican churches. With the exception of Wales, where chapels were, and are, the centre of village life, they were usually built on the periphery, perhaps as a symbol of their non-conformism, or as a result of opposition from steadfast Anglicans.

Churchyards and memorials

For centuries rich and poor were segregated in death much as they were in life. The Victorians maintained this tradition; the wealthy commissioned ornate stone sculptures for their tombstones and organised elaborate funeral processions through the village streets, with black-plumed horses and carriages. The less-well off, having paid their dues to the burial or friendly society, were buried under plain tombstones

following simple ceremonies. Prior to burial, the body would be laid out on the kitchen table in the deceased's cottage, with family and friends keeping watch the night before the funeral. The fate of paupers was almost invariably an unmarked grave.

The country churchyard is a place that has seen little change, apart from the addition of new headstones. Over the centuries it will have risen in height as more burials are inserted. Tranquil, containing dark yews which may be hundreds of years old, and crooked, lichen-encrusted stone memorials, it has become a small oasis for flora and fauna at a time when herbicides and pesticides, along with urban sprawl, have destroyed the natural habitats of many plants and animals. English Nature calculates that Britain lost ninety-eight per cent of its semi-natural grassland within a period of thirty years. Across the country, due to their having been kept apart from the agrarian change on the other side of the wall, churchyards have nurtured their own small patch of bio-diversity; an important ecological factor that was impossible to envisage when the walls surrounding 'God's acre' were first erected.

The twentieth century introduced the stark reality of death on a mass scale, with the impact of the losses sustained in two world wars affecting the whole population. During the First World War in particular, some villages lost a whole generation of young men. In many villages the names of the fallen are recorded on memorials that were normally erected by public subscription to act as a focal point for the remembrance of those who had served and died for their country.

Schools and education

Ewelme School in Oxfordshire, a grammar school founded by Chaucer's granddaughter in 1437, is believed to be the oldest village school in the country. For most rural children,

however, any meaningful form of education did not come until much later; they were regarded as far too important a part of the labour force.

The eighteenth century witnessed the development of dame schools, private establishments run by educated women who charged a small fee, and charity schools financed by endowments, donations and money paid by the child as 'school pence'. If there was no wealthy benefactor to create a new building, the church was often used or classes took place in cottages.

Such schools offered an opportunity for learning to read and write and do simple arithmetic, although the standard achieved by most children was low. Mass illiteracy did not end until the introduction of the Sunday school. Robert Raikes set up the first recorded Sunday school in Gloucester in 1780.

BELOW AND BELOW LEFT: East Dean, East Sussex, in 1921 and today. Memorials stand in many villages to record the names of those who served and died for their country during the First and Second World Wars; they were normally erected by public subscription.

RIGHT: War memorial, Iwerne Minster, Dorset. The twentieth century introduced the stark reality of death on a mass scale, with the impact of the losses sustained during two world wars affecting the whole population and changing rural life for ever.

Held on the one day on which children were not required to work, attendance was free. Lessons covered the three Rs – reading, writing and arithmetic – and lasted all day. In 1785 a non-denominational national organisation, the Sunday School Society, was established.

In 1818 Brougham's Royal Commission reported that only twenty-five per cent of English children received education and half of all adults could not sign their name. Within thirty years, however, three quarters of children were attending Sunday school. By 1870, when William Edward Forster's Education Act introduced full-time elementary education for all children aged five to eleven years, most sizeable villages had their own school, partly financed by the community. The appointment of staff and maintenance of buildings was the joint responsibility of church and village.

Fees of a few pence a week could be charged but were sometimes waived for poorer parents. School attendance was not compulsory. A Victorian engraving depicts children setting off from their honeysuckle-covered cottage towards a thatched schoolhouse, their mother waving a white handkerchief as she watches them, while in the background the village church is depicted to show its continuing influence on the educational life of the child.

In reality, school and rural life in nineteenth century Britain was somewhat harsher. Despite the fact that the Agricultural Children Act, passed in 1873, raised the minimum age of employment to ten, many children were still withdrawn from school at harvest time. The alphabet and basic reading were learnt by repetition and chanting; arithmetical tables, poetry and historic facts were taught by rote, while copperplate handwriting was achieved using copybooks.

Many village schools date from the 1870s and have an adjoining house for the schoolmaster or mistress. The buildings are often of red brick, and the architecture has ecclesiastical elements. A bell was provided to ensured punctuality. Unlike today, when classrooms are covered in children's artwork, the schoolrooms of the past were strikingly bare.

School attendance was made compulsory for all five- to ten-year olds in 1880. Despite this, the records of one

LEFT: The school and village, Hawes, Yorkshire, 1900. A flurry of school building occurred in the latter half of the nineteenth century as a number of acts attempted to establish compulsory attendance for children up to eleven.

BELOW: Ashbury, Oxfordshire, 1919. The architecture of schools often echoed that of ecclesiastical buildings and there was frequently an adjoining house for the schoolmaster or mistress.

The Heart of the Countryside

BELOW: Pilsley, Derbyshire.
The large schoolhouse
reflects Pilsley's past wealth
and civic pride as a thriving
mining village during the
nineteenth and early
twentieth century.

RIGHT AND BELOW RIGHT:
Jessamine Cottage, Eype,
1897 and today. No longer
a tea shop, it is otherwise
remarkably unchanged.

Rural Britain

Nottinghamshire school in 1883 recorded absence due to
turnip singling, carrot weeding, pea pulling and potato picking.
Wall building, goose plucking, inability to pay school fees,
bad feet and the travelling circus are also noted in head
teachers' log books as reasons for non-attendance. Seasonal
excuses included impassable roads in winter, attending to the
harvest in summer and beating for the squire's shoot in
autumn. Disease played a role too, with epidemics sweeping
through families, school classes and whole villages.

The foundations of modern education were laid with
Balfour's Education Act of 1902, which recognised that the
state had an obligation to provide primary and secondary
education for all. Term times and timetables were regulated
in town and country alike, schooling was free and children
could no longer take time off.

The church, a lucky break and education have been cited
as the three routes of escape from poverty. Ironically, advance-
ments in education were a contributory factor in the slow
depopulation of rural areas. Education became the passport
to a new future, and those that left rarely returned. The Butler
Act of 1944 enabled children of the less well-off to stay on at
school while scholarships often allowed access to grammar
school and from there a place at university.

Today, many village schools are
fighting for survival. The average
journey to school is now 5.1 miles
in rural areas, compared to 2.8
miles in urban areas. Few schools
close without a battle and in 1998
Stephen Byers, then minister for
School Standards, announced a
'presumption against closure' of
rural schools, as 'villages lose a
vital focus, families come under
pressure to move, and the knock
on effect on other services sets up
a spiral of decline'.

According to a recent report by
the Local Government Association
on education in rural communities, there are some 2,700
primary schools in England with fewer than 100 pupils, two-
thirds of which are church schools, mainly affiliated to the
Church of England. Seven hundred schools have fewer than
fifty pupils, while in 1999, one school in Lancashire reported
that it had just nine.

The Countryside Agency notes that many village schools
are relatively stable and contribute to the quality of life in the
community. Even so, it is not unusual to find schools contem-
plating diversification so that buildings and resources are
better used. Some raise extra revenue by renting out their
facilities in the evenings for adult education classes such as
fitness, art or embroidery and activities like judo. Sold off and
converted to village halls or day-care centres for the elderly,
they remain a focus of village life; on occasion, redundant
schools become private homes.

Inns and pubs

Inns were originally the hospices, or guest houses, of the
monasteries, often situated in market towns and at key points
along roads. By the eighteenth century, now in private hands,

many had developed into coaching inns. They were a place for travellers to rest and change their mount while also providing overnight accommodation and food. They were expensive to run and standards varied considerably. Staff had to be on hand, stabling provided for fifty horses or more, rooms furnished and kept ready, fresh provisions constantly available. Those well situated would have sufficient trade to prosper; those on less busy roads had a harder time, and many closed when road traffic declined in the wake of the railways' success.

Pubs, originally called alehouses or beerhouses, were private homes where the 'ale wife', who was often a widow, brewed and served the beer for consumption on or off the premises. The Beer House Act of 1830 permitted a householder or ratepayer, on payment of two guineas to the Excise, to turn his private house into a public house. The term 'pub' became common currency soon after. The first licensing legislation – introducing restrictions on opening hours – was passed in 1872.

The pub, unlike the inn, provided no rooms in which to stay. In its parlour and taproom, a wide range of drinks was offered. The parlour was for social gatherings of tradesmen, while the taproom provided a fire and cooking utensils for

Rural Britain

the labouring classes. The pub was very much the village club and it was the only place where labourers could relax in their own company. It was the focal point for gossip; games were played, including darts and dominoes, shove-ha'penny, skittles, cribbage and bar billiards. In 1874, the official figure for consumption of beer was thirty-four gallons a year for every man, woman and child. In Dorset, farm labourers were allowed a gallon of beer each a day, starting with a quart for breakfast at 10 a.m.

The concentration of brewing and growth of tied houses began in the eighteenth century, when small country breweries acquired outlets in market towns and neighbouring villages. During the nineteenth century amalgamations were frequent; by 1914, most pubs were tied to large breweries. As the twentieth century progressed, the breweries' value was measured by the number of tied houses they owned.

The swallowing up of family-owned pubs gradually changed the concept of the pub. Less profitable pubs were

closed, while tenants running the more successful hostelries were removed and replaced by salaried managers. Many pubs, particularly in the 1970s and 1980s, were given a general sprucing up, frequently adopting a corporate style, and the once separate public and saloon bars were often knocked together. The almost invariable result, just as with the clumsy 'restoration' of churches in Victorian times, was loss of character.

More than half of all English villages now have no pub and it is estimated that around six rural pubs close every week in England and Wales. Among the reasons given for closure are young people's preference for larger theme pubs in town, a shift from landlord- to manager-run premises, which require higher profit margins, and greater observance of drink-drive laws.

Pubs provide around 100,000 rural jobs. In addition, the average pub injects at least £64,000 a year into the local economy through its requirements for food and equipment, gardening, decorating, cleaning and the host of other services needed to ensure its smooth running.

The importance of pubs as venues for bringing the community together is emphasised by the recent 'Make the Pub the Hub' campaign, designed to show how breweries and communities can work together to their mutual benefit to help prevent the loss of a vital service. Townspeople are prepared to travel comparatively long distances for good food in a traditional setting, and many country pubs have reinvented themselves as smart restaurants or as 'gastropubs'.

Inn and pub signs represent a huge and colourful open-air exhibition of art which charts history, provides humour and commemorates heroes, villains and much else besides.

They were first used in Roman times, when vine leaves, in honour of Bacchus, were wound round a hoop and fastened to the end of a projecting pole. This sign lasted for centuries. It is mentioned by Chaucer as the 'ale-stake', although the scarcity of vines in some areas meant that ivy or any other greenery was used.

The present-day signboard originated in medieval times, when it became common for alehouses, taverns and inns to have names or distinctive symbols which could be readily recognised by a largely illiterate populace. Richard II, whose badge was the white hart, passed an Act in 1393 obliging innkeepers to provide a prominent sign so that the premises could be identified by the official ale 'conner' or taster, 'otherwise he shall forfeit his ale'. The innkeeper wishing to indicate that his ale had received the approval of the taster attached a garland of greenery and flowers to the sign.

Village pubs often have sporting associations, such as The Cricketers, or trade associations, like The Carpenters' or Masons' Arms. The Plough is common in agricultural areas, while The Nag's Head showed that a horse was for hire. The importance of inns to travellers is indicated by names such as The Travellers' Rest, The Packhorse and The Three Horseshoes, while the once significant wool trade is illustrated in names such as The Woolpack, The Golden Fleece and The Weavers' Arms.

Rural Britain

POST OFFICES

More than any other shop, the post office has come to symbolise the health of a rural community. The majority of post office branches are run, effectively as franchises, by independent businessmen and women within general stores, stationers, petrol stations, pubs, chemists and cafes. In 2003 there were just over 8,000 post offices in communities with less than 10,000 inhabitants. They perform an important social function in rural areas, as many on low incomes do not have bank accounts and cash their benefits there. The Post Office has a team of people across the country, known as rural transfer advisors, whose role is to liaise with local people to maintain a service in their community if the existing branch is under threat.

The first postal service was created by Charles I in 1635 when he made the facilities of the Royal Posts available to the public. Postage was paid by the addressee on delivery. The earliest post offices were usually housed at inns and were known as letter receiving houses; by the 1800s, post offices had frequently been established in a room in the postmaster's own house. Mail was passed through the window to the street, and in some cases postmasters employed their own servants to deliver letters.

The system employed today began in 1840, when Rowland Hill introduced the penny post. Postage, based on weight regardless of distance, was paid by the sender using adhesive postage stamps or stamped stationery.

Contracts for running village post offices were first offered in the 1840s and 1850s, and the first roadside pillar boxes were installed in 1853. In 1872, uniforms were issued to postmen, at that time still known as letter carriers. In the major towns the Post Office was represented by a full-time postmaster. In the smaller towns and villages, this role was taken on by a sub-postmaster who was not generally salaried but instead, like today, ran a shop or other businesses from the same premises.

Much business involved the sale of money or postal orders, which were a common method of sending money by post before cheques. The Post Office savings bank opened in 1861 and from 1865 offices also dealt with annuities and life insurance. A telegraph was operated from 1870 with messenger boys delivering the telegrams. It was the only means of rapid communication before the introduction of the telephone.

Bicycles were officially introduced in 1896 and in 1919 the Post Office bought its own motorised vehicle fleet; today the cheerful red of the post office van is a common and welcome sight, delivering to outlying farms and cottages. Postmen serve an important social role in rural areas, since they are frequently the most regular visitors of the poor and elderly and are the first to notice when something is wrong.

LETTERS

North Woolton.
POST OFFICE.

Village halls

Village halls follow closely behind the pub and church in their importance as meeting places. Like reading rooms and playing fields, many were provided by philanthropic members of the gentry during the nineteenth century.

Church halls, schools, barns, stables, cottages and later former RAF and army huts were all converted for use as village halls. A single-roomed building might start out as a Sunday school, become a reading room, then a village hall. Reading rooms were an attempt to dissuade farm labourers from leaving the land in pursuit of work in the towns and included diversions like bagatelle tables. Village clubs also developed in the late nineteenth century, usually for men only, providing snooker and billiards.

Some village halls are named after the benefactor who financed them, or after Victoria and Albert; others have been funded by public subscription or constructed with the aid of government grants. Since its foundation by the Carnegie Corporation in the early 1930s, the Carnegie UK Trust has given grants totalling more than £24 million to villages, funding the development of halls and public libraries. These grants have helped promote rural arts, heritage and social welfare. A more recent spur was the Millennium; many communities chose to mark the event by raising money to build a new hall or renovate one that was run down.

Over half the halls are more than sixty years old and some are listed. Architecturally, nineteenth-century halls reflect the brick-built characteristics of contemporary houses and schools. They often have a porch, a slate roof, open ceilings, exposed beams and sash windows.

During the Second World War, many village halls were used for civil defence training and to entertain troops. They remain essential to rural life and many small voluntary and community organisations depend on them. They are, in addition, the first port of call during emergencies such as floods and snowstorms. Overall usage has increased during the past ten years and over 300 different activities were recorded in the 1998 Village Halls Survey. The hall is the place where the community comes together for activities such as yoga classes, sports, parties, amateur dramatics, luncheon clubs and meetings of the horticultural society. They are also used as day centres and polling stations. In recent years it has become clear that they can also play a part-time role as shops, post

offices or even doctor's surgeries; some are being used as IT resource centres and for computer training.

A survey conducted by the National Federation of Woman's Institutes in 1999s reported a thriving network of village halls, with ninety per cent of respondents reporting that they had one, compared with fifty-four per cent in 1950. Around 240 new halls had been constructed and a further 216 refurbished or improved. There are currently around

The Heart of the Countryside

9,000 halls in rural England, representing the largest network of community facilities, second only to churches. They are now largely financed by local authorities, with local fund-raising contributing an extra £7.5 million a year; most are run by a small committee of volunteers representing local user organisations and villagers.

Village shops

In an age when branded pre-packaged products fill the shelves of village shop and supermarket alike it is hard to imagine a time when quantities of tea, sugar and many other provisions were weighed out individually for each customer. Within living memory of many villagers, however, this was the case.

Village shops were rare until the early nineteenth century. Everyday foodstuffs were still largely produced and prepared at home. The gentry had their own farms and dairies and were mostly self-sufficient in grain, meat, dairy produce, poultry,

eggs and vegetables. Tenant farmers lived mostly off their own produce, and also provided labourers with what they needed. Cottagers with large gardens or allotments sold or exchanged their surplus produce, sometimes employing a higgler to take it to town and sell it on their behalf. Some kept chickens and sold eggs. Others baked cakes and pies to sell to their neighbours.

Many household necessities were bought from travelling peddlers or hawkers who, long after the establishment of village shops, were still a common sight trudging between the hedgerows along rutted and muddy country lanes. At the time of the 1871 census there were some 45,000 of these itinerants, who bought their wares in the cities and towns to sell on to the country people for a small profit. Peddlers carried small items like ribbons, thread and cheap jewellery in a basket or a box-cum-display cabinet, while hawkers brokered larger items such as ironmongery, crockery, pots and pans. Villagers were also visited by Gypsies, who sold everything from clothes pegs to brooms, as well as by knife grinders, chair-menders and travelling tailors.

The arrival of the first mass-produced factory-made goods via the developing railway network made change inevitable.

From the 1830s to the 1870s entrepreneurial shopkeepers in the villages seized the opportunity to stock the new and cheaper products, promoting the consumption of former luxuries like tea, coffee and sugar, as well as non-perishable foodstuffs and household goods. By the 1880s they were supplying the cottagers with many of their requirements. However, while these might have appeared to be halcyon

71

days, the future of the village shop was already in jeopardy. The transport links that brought goods in also allowed customers to travel to shops in the larger towns and cities, while the younger generation was lured away by the 'bright lights', where higher wages could be earned.

The Saturday shopping excursion to the nearest town became a regular activity, and competition, from supermarkets in particular, hastened the decline of the village shop in the twentieth century. The 222,000 grocery shops that existed in 1950 have dwindled to 35,000 today. In 2000 it was estimated that seventy-two per cent of villages had no shop. The survey conducted by the National Federation of Woman's Institutes identified the loss of over 1,000 individual village shops in the previous ten years. In addition, numerous post offices, butchers, banks or building societies, greengrocers and a host of other shops from hairdressers to newsagents had also gone. It ranked the desire for a new shop as the fourth most important improvement that members wished to see.

Running a village shop is seen by many as a vocation but there are few who willingly buy into the long hours and small rewards that such businesses offer. By the 1980s, with retirement looming for many stalwart shopkeepers, there was little option but to sell up, with the inevitability that the shop would be turned into a private house. Over recent years, the pressure on such businesses has been compounded by taxation and onerous health and safety regulations. Often, it is only when a shop has gone that local people realise how much they have depended upon it, with the effects felt most keenly by those who are constrained by lack of transport, such as the elderly, young parents and teenagers.

Closure is, however, not inevitable. Some shops have survived through diversification, in many cases stocking goods formerly sold by those that have closed. The more entrepreneurial have re-established home deliveries. Traditional milk rounds have diversified to supply everything from bread to fizzy drinks, while individual traders deliver fresh fish, boxes of organic vegetables and even meals for the freezer, in a manner reminiscent of the days when the baker's boy would go round the village on a bike.

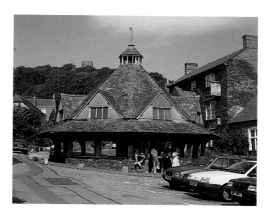

BELOW AND RIGHT: Dunster, Somerset, the market house c 1880 and today. The wooden yarn market, built in 1609 is a memorial to the town's heritage as a thriving manufacturer of cloth and local commercial centre. A market has been held on the site every Friday since the Middle Ages.

BELOW AND BELOW RIGHT: Crawley, West Sussex, the fair in 1905 and today. Many county towns still have a regular market day; most are for the sale of clothes, bric-a-brac and fruit and vegetables rather than livestock.

RIGHT: Bideford, Devon, 1907. A visit to the weekly markets offered items unobtainable in the village.

FOLLOWING PAGES: Settle, Yorkshire, 1921. The central marketplace was the social and commercial hub of most small towns. Market day was a chance to do business, meet old friends and perhaps make a few new ones.

Rural Britain

The most positive outcomes have occurred where communities have taken on the challenge of forming a co-operative. By providing services jointly through one outlet, economies of scale and effort can be achieved that benefit both those running the shop and the customer who only has to visit one location. There are grants to help with such projects, along with advice from organisations such as the Village Retail Services Association (ViRSA).

One major supermarket chain is aiming to help keep rural shops sustainable by allowing them to sell non-perishable proprietary and branded products bought from its stores. Members of the scheme can shop as normal customers but with extra benefits that include access to merchandising and marketing assistance in order to help promote the goods.

Market towns

While some villages had a weekly market in the square or on the green it was common to walk a distance of anything up to ten miles to visit the market in the nearby town. The need to travel such distances on foot was taken for granted by country people, despite the fact that the journey was often along roads and byways deep in mud and choked at times with those bringing in their goods and livestock for sale.

Market towns, many of them former villages that had expanded as a result of their closeness to major roads, have always been a vital part of the rural community. Market day was a chance to do business, meet old friends and perhaps make new ones. It was also the day when the shops of the town

could be visited in order to purchase items unobtainable in the village.

In most towns, to allow stalls and pens to be set up, market day involved closing off entire streets which soon came alive with cattle, sheep, goats and hens, as well as milling crowds. The result was a rich mixture of scents, sights and sounds, with the auctioneer shouting his rapid, and to the outsider seemingly unintelligible, chant above the din and confusion.

Many county towns still have a regular market day; most are for the sale of clothes, bric-a-brac and fruit and vegetables

rather than livestock. Encouragingly, there has been a recent return to the concept of the country market through the creation of farmers' markets at which farmers and small producers sell everything from bread and honey to meat and cheese. They represent a high-profile shop window for the British farming industry and offer a low-cost entry point for many farmers who have not sold direct to the public before. The idea began with a single market in 1997 and has grown to be a thriving industry in its own right, with some 450 markets in virtually every area of the country, earning producers a total of £166 million a year.

The rapid rise of these markets reflects consumers' desire for produce that reflects ethical farming practices and is both local and traceable. It also represents a reaction to global agribusiness and to the impersonality of supermarkets. Since all the products have been grown, reared, caught, brewed, pickled, baked, smoked or processed by the stallholder, the customer can be confident of the origin, quality and freshness of the foods. Farmers and growers are also able to communicate directly with their customers – at sixty per cent of markets the majority are regulars – gaining invaluable feedback as well as income.

GREENS & SQUARES

Often one of the main public elements of the village, the green or square is all that remains of the extensive common land before enclosure. In many villages it constitutes the focal point of the road pattern.

The green was where the commercial and leisure activities of the village, including markets and fairs, were held, as can be seen from the presence of old market crosses. In some villages a cross stood even if there was no market, as it was, until their abolition following the Reformation, a central station for religious processions, when villagers walked round the village at Rogation. The green was where the maypole was erected to celebrate the festivities of May Day. It was on the green, also, that wrongdoers were humiliated in the stocks.

From about 1830, at a time when large tracts of common land were being enclosed, many small areas were allocated specially 'for the exercise and recreation of the inhabitants'. Within the Commons Registration Act 1965 a green is defined as either 'land set out under any Act or Award for the recreation of the inhabitants' or 'land subject to customary right of playing lawful sports or pastimes, evidenced by at least 20 years exercise of the right'.

Over the course of the years, many greens have disappeared under housing. A recent initiative by the Countryside Agency provides grants to help both rural and urban communities, with little outdoor community space, to create a 'doorstep green'.

ABOVE: Richmond, North Yorkshire. Fairs still add local colour when they are set up in the square.

RIGHT: Godstone, Surrey c 1955. Cricket on the green, a social and sporting scene that has changed little over the years.

FOLLOWING PAGES: Aldborough, Yorkshire, 1907. The green was frequently a focus for commercial and leisure activities, including markets and fairs, as indicated by the presence of old market crosses.

RIGHT: Dufton, Cumbria. The Georgian village pump is now a landmark but was once a necessity when few houses had their own water supply.

LEFT: 'Elderslie', Ockley, 1906. Country houses were once the lynch-pin of local communities, providing work and a social focus.
BELOW: Prideaux Place, Padstow, Cornwall, 1888. Inside the big house there was continuity and order; many contained fine collections of paintings, furniture and porcelain and today are open to the public.

RIGHT: Bodysgallen Hall, Llandudno, Gwynedd, Wales. Many great houses were eventually sold off by the families that had owned them for generations and they became schools, company headquarters, nursing homes or, as in this case, hotels.

Rural Britain

The big house

Often glimpsed between trees or hedges although physically separated from the village by imposing iron gates and a long drive, the big house was, for centuries, an integral part of rural life. Prior to the twentieth century it frequently represented the largest single source of employment within the community, employing numerous domestic and garden staff. The house of the local squire or member of the gentry was often quite grand, although on a smaller scale than the great house or stately home owned by the aristocracy.

Many Victorian squires aspired to the paternal ideal, indulging in good works as well as offering employment, and the house and its grounds would be opened once or twice a year for fetes and teas. Their wives visited the poor and sick and did charitable works. They expected, and received, deference. The nouveau riche industrialists, bankers and shopkeepers who acquired property in the country also aspired to this lifestyle. Reaching into deep pockets, they remodelled and built. Construction of houses reached a peak during this period, with almost as many new houses created as in the previous three centuries.

Those that lived in the house and grounds formed a community in their own right, and through the grapevine villagers were always kept up to date with what was going on 'up at the big house'. Inside the house there was continuity and order. Organisation was often almost military in its precision and the hierarchy of servants was clear-cut. Everyone knew their place; it was a world of 'upstairs' and 'downstairs' with ties between the families of the gentry and those of the servants sometimes going back generations.

The standing of the head gardener was on a par with that of the butler. In larger establishments his role was almost entirely administrative. He organised his staff and educated them in the art and use of manure, glasshouses, frames and pits. His chief responsibility was the provision of top quality produce for the kitchen. Fruit and vegetables were grown in the walled kitchen garden where considerable ingenuity was employed to extend the growing season and increase the range of fresh produce that could be brought to the table.

The big house had its origins in the medieval manor. Derived from manoir, the French word for dwelling, the manor comprised the whole estate of a manorial lord, usually a gentleman or knight rather than one of the higher nobles. Tenure, in the centuries immediately following the Conquest, was granted by the king in exchange for military service. It was later commuted to rent.

The manor was an economic unit and the lord both owned and built the houses for his workers. A manor might contain several villages. Conversely, a village might be divided into several manors, each with its own manor house. The lord would not necessarily be in residence, in which case he would leave a bailiff in charge. Villeins, who farmed strips in

the common fields, owed service to the lord, working on his land for part of the week.

In the early medieval period, the big house was often fortified. It had a lofty open hall where the moot, or court of justice, was held fortnightly, the focal point of social as well as administrative activity in the village. The lord's chamber was over service rooms at one end.

One of the standard patterns for large medieval houses was the characteristic H-plan. This consisted of a hall with a two-storey block at each end, with extra rooms for retainers and guests. In the rash of building following the Dissolution of the Monasteries, the big house expanded; more rooms had fireplaces, so the roof had several chimneys, often ornamented. The appearance of the house became architectural, so that it was readily distinguishable not only in scale but in style from the other houses in the village, which were built in the local vernacular. By the nineteenth century, many houses were square in plan, the front door opening into a small hall with formal rooms on either side and the service rooms at the back, with the servants occupying the attic and basement.

The great houses, until the end of the fifteenth century, were the large castles, such as Windsor, Arundel or Alnwick. They were the power centres of the great nobles. With the consequent reduction in the need for fortified, defensive structures following the end of the Wars of the Roses, they were replaced in the Tudor and Elizabethan periods by grand, ostentatious houses; Longleat and Montacute are notable examples. The late seventeenth and early eighteenth centuries saw the creation of palatial houses like Chatsworth and Blenheim, supervised by architects of the calibre of Talman, Vanbrugh and Hawksmoor, and built in the classical style. Their layout was designed to meet both the requirements of family life as well as the provision of constant hospitality and entertainment. Great attention was also lavished on their extensive landscaped grounds.

The Victorian country house, often neo-gothic in style, was the culmination of this tradition. Huge and rambling, it contained as many as a hundred rooms. A typical ground floor might have a hall, dining-room, luncheon-room, drawing-room, billiard-room, smoking-room, morning-

room, business-room, study, library, various service rooms and the kitchen. There might be several staircases, each reserved for a different category of people. The social life of the upper classes revolved around parties held in these houses, with organised shooting and fishing.

The great agricultural depression of the last quarter of the century, combined with the introduction of death duties in 1894, sapped the wealth and power of the gentry and aristocracy. The First World War saw many of their young men die in the mud of Flanders. Between 1918 and 1922, a quarter of the landed property in Britain changed hands. During the inter-war period domestic service ceased to be an attractive option for many villagers, and by the end of the Second World War, the old way of life had gone.

For many country houses, including great houses, the outlook was bleak, with demolition frequently the solution chosen by embattled families. In terms of the loss to British architecture, what followed has been compared to the destruction that occurred with the Dissolution of the Monasteries. It is estimated that 1,300 major country houses were wholly or partly destroyed in the period between 1875 and 1975.

It was thanks to the National Trust, which was established in 1895, that many of the great houses survived. In the mid-1930s, it realised that they were threatened with something close to extinction so it devised the 'Country House Scheme' with the aim of saving such properties for future generations. As a result, Britain has some magnificent houses that are open to the public, bringing in many thousands of visitors and tourists, and boosting the rural economy.

Where families were successful in selling off a house it frequently became a school, hotel, company headquarters or nursing home. In recent years, many of these have, in turn, been put up for sale by their institutional owners; they are again becoming homes, as developers divide and convert them into prestigious apartments, often also building luxury houses in the grounds, with the result that new communities are being created.

The Heart of
the Countryside

LEFT: Mechanisation has made the jobs involved in maintaining large estates, including hedge-cutting, less labour intensive.

BELOW: Penny Hill Park, Bagshot, Surrey, 1906. Villagers often found employment in the extensive landscaped grounds of the big house.

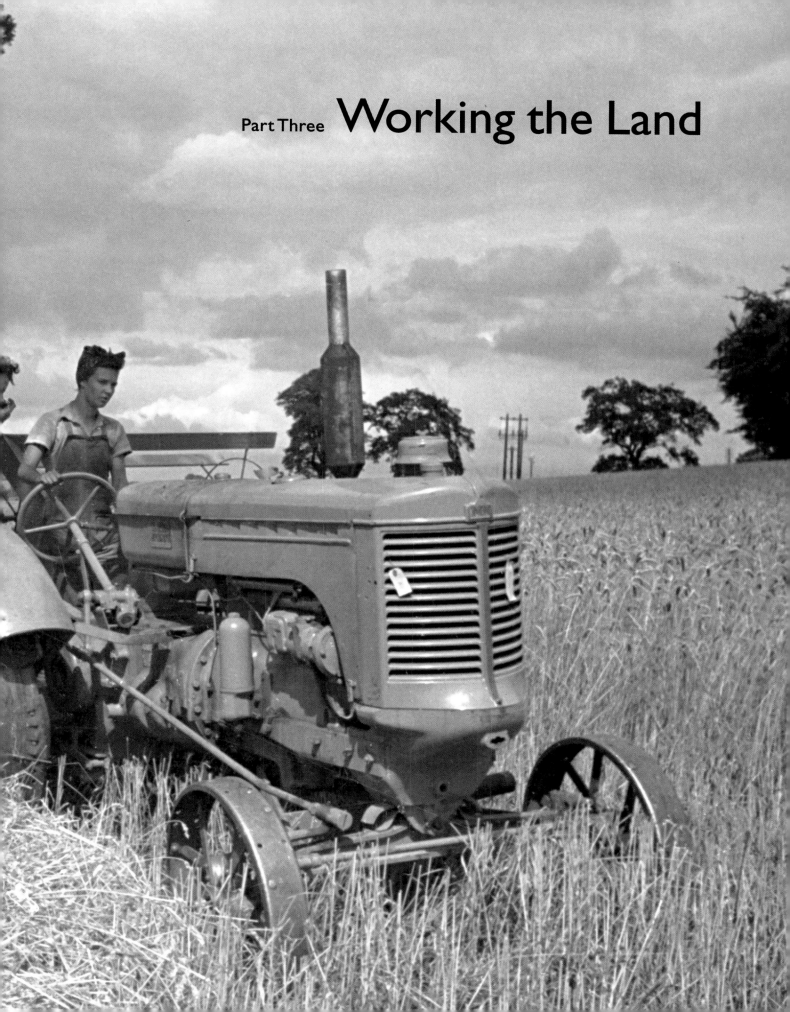

Part Three Working the Land

PREVIOUS PAGES: Women help to bring in the harvest, 1943. A Women's Land Army of nearly 200,000 took the place of men who had been called up to fight during the Second World War. The need to maintain war-time food production, and to feed a burgeoning post-war population forced the pace of mechanisation.

BELOW: Moretonhampstead, Devon, 1918. Nearly three million extra acres were brought under the plough during World War One.

BELOW: Hadrian's Wall,
Northumberland. Heaths,
moorland and common
grazing land have all been
transformed by the graphic
lines of walls and hedging.
While there is evidence of
the use of walls since prehistoric times for defensive
and religious purposes,
their use for farming dates
first to the Middle Ages
when land was increasingly
enclosed for agriculture.

*Working
the Land*

From the moment man first roamed across the diverse and fascinating landscape of the place we now call Britain, the countryside has served to provide the food and materials required for human life to be sustained. In time, the random foraging of the early hunter gatherers turned to a more exploitative existence as the people of the Neolithic period set up farmsteads and utilized the qualities offered by the varying underlying geologies to grow crops and graze livestock.

Few places remain that have not in some way been changed by the human hand, be it rolling hill or verdant woodland; yet, just for a moment, it is still possible to imagine the bustle of modern life being suspended. We may still marvel at a landscape that has a natural beauty even though the early morning mist rises from what are essentially man-made features: hedge bounded trackways, mirrored millponds and rolling, plough rutted fields.

Much of the pattern of today's landscape was already established by late Saxon times. However, it also carries the distinctive stamp of the enclosure movement, which reached its peak in the eighteenth and nineteenth centuries, when great swathes of countryside were redefined with hedges and dry stone walls.

The natural rhythms of the countryside are played out across a scene that changes with the seasons as farmers and workers toil in all weathers, caring for animals, tilling the soil, scattering seed and harvesting crops while, around them, the air is infused with the scents of nature.

The turmoil that has swept across the rural scene has been immense: epidemics, famine, drought, blight, civil war, economic slump and rural unemployment. Yet, through it all,

the land and those who work it have endeavoured to answer the nation's needs.

Farmers perpetuate skills first learnt in ancient times to secure harvests of corn, timber, fruit, and a host of other produce. In so doing they are guardians and managers of over seventy-five per cent of the land area of Britain. Without them the landscape would rapidly become choked with weeds and scrub, the ecological balance upset. While the countryside is still a place for producing food it is also one of the most important aspects of our heritage and there is an increasing determination to maintain it and to protect the environment and wildlife within it.

There are, however, many conflicts. Farmers struggle with European Union bureaucracy, planning restrictions and the drive for sustainable practices and greater public access, while many subsidies are dependent on adopting methods that some feel are inconsistent with good farming and land management.

Old photographs of farmers and agricultural labourers reveal that, until comparatively recently, these men and

women had the gnarled weather-beaten look that comes from being constantly exposed to wind, sun and rain. While it remains a rigorous life, today's farm workers have some comfort and protection, since they are likely to spend at least part of their life inside the cab of a tractor. Despite the frustrations and hardships, those involved are often perceived as enjoying the good life, perhaps because, in our bones, this is where our roots lie.

Years of change

Throughout Victoria's reign the number of farmers remained relatively constant. They ranged from aristocratic landowners with vast estates to comfortable squires and – forming ninety per cent of the total – tenant farmers. Whatever their status, their role in keeping alive the rural economy was central; they gave employment to huge numbers of labourers and domestic servants and used the services of the village craftsmen and tradesmen.

With the repeal of the Corn Laws in 1846, which had banned imports until domestically produced grain reached a certain price, there was a fear that depression would come to farming. In fact, the 1850s and 1860s saw Victorian agriculture enjoy something of a golden age. This was a period of high returns, with the introduction of improved breeds and

crops, fertilisers, and the replacement of wood by iron in the manufacture of many agricultural implements. There was a greater use of scientific methods. Steam power was increasingly applied to ploughing, threshing and winnowing. The amount of arable land gradually declined, giving way to pasture; mixed farming increased as crops and livestock were integrated. In 1860, eighty per cent of food consumed was still produced domestically. By 1870, a greater acreage of land was under the plough than at any time before or since.

However, five years later, farming took an abrupt turn for the worse, initiating a period which was to become known as the Great Depression. Between 1875 and 1882 there were six years of bad weather, leading to poor harvests and other agricultural calamities. Flooding caused devastation to arable farming. There was an epidemic of liver rot in sheep in Somerset, North Dorset and Lincolnshire, resulting in the deaths of four million animals. There were several instances of cattle plague in the 1870s and an outbreak of foot-and-mouth disease from 1881 to 1883.

Meanwhile, the continuing rise in the population led to an increased volume of imports of grain from the USA, Canada and Australia. The rapid development of railways within the USA enabled producers in the prairies to send their grain to market quickly and cheaply, while its export in steamships instead of under sail further helped to lower costs. Without the protection of the Corn Laws, British agriculture was

LEFT: Farmland, near
Chepstow, Gwent, South
Wales. World markets as
well as domestic needs
now shape Britain's rural
landscape. Traditional
crops such as wheat and
potatoes are now grown
alongside oilseed rape and
sugarbeet, both of which
are farmed for export.

BELOW: Straw bailing, Dorset.
Previously a community
activity, cutting and
gathering in the harvest
has now become a solitary
job. Mechanisation has
streamlined agricultural
processes, drastically
reducing the number of
farmworkers needed to
complete tasks.

incredibly vulnerable. The prices of wheat and wool, which had been the bedrock of English and Welsh prosperity since the thirteenth century, declined by half between the 1870s and the mid-1880s. By 1885 the area under wheat had shrunk by a million acres, and Britain was importing sixty-five per cent of its needs.

Life had always been difficult for agricultural labourers; their condition now became increasingly desperate. Some were able to acquire peasant smallholdings when farms were broken up, but most suffered. Crofters in the Highlands were subsisting on as little as £8 a year. In the south, the pace of rural depopulation, which had begun in the eighteenth century, began to quicken. Countless labourers left the country for factory work in the towns. Often accompanied by large families, few could read or write, and many did not know how to buy a railway ticket to the town where they were seeking work.

Between 1871 and 1881 the number of working farm labourers dropped by nearly 100,000. Within twenty years only twelve per cent of employed men worked on the land; Britain was now reliant on its empire for food. By the time the storm clouds of the First World War broke across Europe, British farming had reached a parlous state. The walls and hedges were poorly maintained, farm buildings were crumbling, while the land itself was poorly managed and unproductive. Death duties, introduced in 1894, dealt a hammer blow to many landowners and countless long established families, which had held their estates for centuries, were forced to sell their lands.

In 1914 Britain was only producing one-third of the food it needed, so radical action was required; two years later War Agricultural Executive Committees were set up. Measures implemented included a minimum price for wheat and minimum wages for labourers. Nearly three million extra acres were brought under the plough and smallholdings, as well as urban allotments, were encouraged.

However, the respite did not last long. After 1920, prices slumped as cheap imports again flooded into the country. Most of the newly created arable land reverted to pasture and land prices fell drastically. While subsidies, grants, quotas and tariffs were introduced during the 1930s, the industry in 1939 was still largely derelict and under-capitalised with a third fewer agricultural workers than thirty years earlier.

However, as in 1914, it was war that helped to regenerate British agriculture. With the start of the Second World War derelict land was reclaimed and the arable acreage increased by over six million. A Women's Land Army of some 200,000 took the place of men who had been called up to fight. This was a turning point in farming practice for it forced the pace of mechanisation. The horse was superseded by the tractor in the desperate struggle to feed a population of some fifty million.

Working the Land

HEDGES

The use of hedges to delineate land boundaries is ancient. They appear to have been used by the Romans, while some hedges dating from the Anglo-Saxon period still survive. Between 1750 and 1850 enclosing farmers and landowners planted around 200,000 miles of hedges, as many as in the previous 500 years. They also built mile upon mile of stone walls and in the process created a striking patchwork pattern that is still etched on the landscape, despite the widespread uprooting of many hedgerows in recent decades.

Hedges vary considerably in design depending on local traditions, the plants available and the type of livestock enclosed. When laid well they create a formidably strong barrier, providing animals with shelter from wind and rain and shade from the sun. They also serve as a windbreak for crops and provide a habitat for birds, insects and other wildlife, while supplying food in the form of nuts and berries.

Modern methods of hedge-laying date from the late 1700s, with hawthorn the most common hedging tree. Stems are partly cut through and bent over diagonally ('plashing') and intertwined with other stems. In this way they continue to grow. Stakes are inserted through the hedge at intervals and the tops are woven together with thin rods, generally of hazel. Hedges require active management to stay in good condition.

ABOVE: Meikleour, Perthshire, Scotland, 1947. A forestry worker trims the world's tallest and longest hedge, planted in 1746. Trimmed once every ten years, the beech hedge has been described as one of the arboreal wonders of the world – its tapered height varies from 24.4 m (80 ft) to 36.6 m (120 ft) along its length of 550 m (1,804 ft).

RIGHT: Sherbourne, Gloucestershire, 1964. A farmer lays part of a 3/4-mile-long hedge using a billhook. Modern methods of hedge-laying date from the late 1700s with hawthorn the most common hedging tree.

LEFT: Hedgelaying, Oxfordshire. Hedging is usually carried out in winter. The hedgelayer partly cuts through the stems and bends them diagonally; properly done, the sap will continue to rise through the uncut branches, keeping the hedge alive and strong.

BELOW: Milford, Surrey, c 1955. Animal power was employed since the earliest times. Oxen were used until the late nineteenth century, while a wide variety of farm machinery continued to be powered by horses until well within living memory.

BELOW: Llanddona, Isle of Anglesey, Wales, c 1955. Horse-drawn machines for cutting grass first became widespread in the 1870s. In many places further mechanisation was adopted only when the old ways became unviable due to the rising cost of labour and the need to feed a growing population.

RIGHT: Shapwick, Somerset, 1904. Cutting peat for fuel on the Somerset Levels and Moors probably dates back to Roman times. The turfing took place between April and September when the ground was at its driest. The 1960s saw a surge in the use of peat for horti-culture which led to large scale extraction through the use of machinery.

LEFT: John Fowler and Company Engineers' straw-burning steam ploughing engine, Leeds, West Yorkshire, 1874. Steam traction engines were in widespread use by the 1860s, although they were generally found to be viable only for a minority of farmers whose fields were large enough to justify the expense.

BELOW: Kirton, Lincolnshire, 1907. The introduction of steam-powered threshing machines changed the rituals of both harvesting and haymaking. The sheaves of corn were pitched up to a man atop the threshing machine who would feed them into the spinning threshing drum. The corn poured from chutes into sacks while straw and chaff were disgorged separately.

RIGHT: Following their development in the USA in the 1890s, tractors employing internal combustion engines first appeared on British farms during the First World War and, by 1921, some 20,000 were in use.

Mechanisation

Working the Land

Animal power had been employed since the earliest times. Oxen were used until the late nineteenth century, while a wide variety of farm machinery continued to be powered by horses until well within living memory.

Mechanisation began in earnest in the eighteenth century, with Jethro Tull's invention of the seed drill in 1701. Andrew Meikle adapted steam for threshing in 1786 and steam threshing remained a common sight until the late 1940s. Steam traction engines for ploughing were initially developed in the 1830s and were in widespread use by the 1860s, although they were generally found to be viable only for a minority of farmers whose fields were large enough to justify the expense. The most effective system involved the plough being pulled back and forth across the field on a cable between two engines, one on either side of the field.

In the 1870s horse-drawn machines for cutting grass became widespread. By 1890 around eighty per cent of the British corn acreage was cut this way. Following their development in the USA in the 1890s, tractors employing internal combustion engines first appeared on British farms during the First World War. By 1921 some 20,000 were employed, with the figure rising to around 60,000 by 1939 and 480,000 by 1956. Perhaps inevitably, the design of early tractors was based on that of horse-drawn carts. Harry Ferguson invented a three-point linkage system which meant that farm implements such as ploughs could be mounted on a hydraulic arm behind the tractor, enabling it to back right up to hedges and leave far less unworked land at the margins of fields.

Farm electrification began hesitantly in the 1920s, not becoming significant until after 1945, with eighty-five per cent of farms connected by the 1960s.

Post-war developments

The need to feed a growing population after the war, coupled with the rising cost of labour, led to radical changes in farming

97

BELOW: Harvesting, 1929. Combine harvesters that could cut and thresh barley in one action meant that instead of taking weeks the harvest could now be completed within days.

RIGHT: South Carlton, Lincolnshire, 1919. A General Ordnance tractor and plough at the International Tractor Trials. The design of early tractors was based on that of horse-drawn carts; the invention of a three-point linkage system meant that farm implements such as ploughs could be mounted on a hydraulic arm behind the tractor, enabling it to back right up to hedges.

FAR RIGHT: Crickley Barrow, Gloucestershire, 1956. Farm workers use a combine harvester to thresh out the seeds from cocksfoot, a perennial grass. Changes in the types of crop grown, as well as increases in intensity of farming spurred the development of new machinery and multitasking machines.

practice. Crop rotation was abandoned in favour of mono-cultures, requiring the use of increasingly potent chemicals to kill weeds and to suppress disease. Imported fertilisers, subsidised by the government, replaced manure.

In tandem with the new intensive farming, mechanisation advanced apace. Hedges were uprooted to facilitate the movement of combine harvesters and other large machines across the newly created prairies. Poultry and pigs were reared intensively in large, specially constructed buildings. By 1970, around 100 million chickens a year were spending their, increasingly brief, lives in battery cages.

As a result, Britain's dependence on imported food was considerably reduced, certainly it was much less than it had been for much of the period prior to 1945. Entry into the European Economic Community (now the European Union) in 1973 meant that imports from countries outside the Community – often Commonwealth countries like Australia – were blocked by high levies imposed by the Common Agricultural Policy (CAP). However, this attempt to support European farmers led to over-production of certain crops, resulting in notorious grain 'mountains' and wine 'lakes'.

The 1992 reform of the CAP aimed to overcome this by taking land out of production and compensating farmers for their loss of income in a process called set-aside. Now the CAP encourages non-agricultural development that creates jobs in other sectors, such as travel and tourism. Under the Countryside Access Scheme instituted in 2000, farmers in the UK can create footpaths on set-aside land to enable people to visit sites which are either of historical interest or are of outstanding natural beauty.

Today, farming is still a vital part of the economy, employing half a million people and providing more than half the country's food. Almost a third of the total area of Britain's agricultural land is managed by tenant farmers. Most are small family farms; the predominance of agribusiness notwithstanding, they comprise some of the industry's most successful businesses. This has, however, been accompanied by a considerable reduction in the labour force, which is now only a third of what it was in 1946. The pace of technological change has been relentless; a harvest that would once have taken weeks can now be completed within days by a combine harvester.

Harvesting and haymaking

Harvest-time remains a critical point in the year, with the farmer finally able to assess whether or not his efforts have been rewarded. It is also one of the most worrying times in the farming calendar as much depends on the weather and on the farmer's ability to gather in the crop at precisely the right time.

In previous centuries the grain harvest was an event that involved the participation of the whole community, including women and children. The crop was first bound into sheaves; four or five of these would then be stacked into stooks. When sufficiently dry these would be piled onto wagons and taken to the barn. While the work was hard, not to mention hot and dusty, it was also something of a social occasion, frequently attended by ritual, with the last ears of corn in the field carefully cut and made into a corn dolly.

Haymaking also involved considerable labour. It generally lasted two or three weeks as the cut grass had to be turned and fluffed by hand using wooden rakes and pitchforks in order to dry it. Once dry, it was loaded into carts and taken to be built into stacks which were then thatched with straw. This covering allowed the stacks to be kept for a number of years without risk of deterioration.

The introduction of steam-powered threshing machines changed the rituals of both harvesting and haymaking. The sheaves of corn were thrown up to a man on top of the threshing machine who would feed them into the spinning threshing drum. The corn poured out of chutes into sacks while straw and chaff came out separately.

The arrival of the combine harvester further reduced the need for human participation. In common usage in America by the 1920 and '30s, they only came into use in Britain during the 1940s. The corn no longer needed to be cut and left to dry in the fields. Instead, the machine combined the threshing and winnowing processes, discharging the grain into a hopper so that it could be taken back to the farmyard to be artificially dried and stored. Meanwhile, the straw expelled from the rear was baled using another machine.

LEFT: Sibford Ferris, Oxfordshire. In the post-war years mechanisation advanced apace. Hedges were uprooted to facilitate the movement of combine harvesters and other large machines, such as this tractor and harrow, across the newly created prairies.

BELOW: Nocton Fen, Lincolnshire. The modern harvest involves the efforts of just a few workers and leaves the fields tidy with the bales ready to be collected mechanically. Round bales are increasingly preferred to square, as they reduce the time and cost of moving straw from the fields into storage.

BELOW: Coltishall, Norfolk, 1902. The crop was first bound into sheaves which were then stacked into stooks. When sufficiently dry, these would be piled onto wagons and taken to the barn and later threshed using a hand flail.

RIGHT: South Walsham, Norfolk, 1902. The harvest was once an event that involved the participation of the whole community, including women and children. The work was hard, not to mention hot and dusty, but it was also something of a social occasion.

BELOW: Sheep dipping, Cenarth, Dyfed, Wales, c 1965. The wool industry was once a key contributor to England's prosperity but declined when first cotton and then synthetic fibres replaced wool in the manufacture of cloth.

RIGHT: North York Moors National Park. Today wool accounts for only three per cent of world fibre production and sheep are reared almost entirely for their meat. A third of the EU's production of lamb and mutton is based in Britain, with around twenty-one million breeding ewes.

FAR RIGHT: Aberglaslyn, Gwynedd, Wales, 1913. In the days before motor cars it was common to find animals being driven along country lanes from one part of a farm to another or even to market.

Rural Britain

Dairying and livestock

Prior to the development of the railway network in the nineteenth century, the average farm kept only two or three cows. Well into the century it was not unusual to see the milkmaid on her three-legged stool attending to the milking in the field or farmyard. Most farms had a dairy run by the farmer's wife who made milk, butter and cream for domestic consumption. Cheese-making required more equipment and was not so widely undertaken. However, cheeses were less perishable and thus lucrative products and, in the seventeenth and eighteenth centuries, a considerable trade developed.

Milk was often bought direct from a milkman leading the cow from door to door, or from a milkman or milkmaid

carrying pails suspended from a yoke mounted on their shoulders. Later, large tin churns were taken round by pony and trap. The railways made it possible to transport milk quickly to urban areas and, as demand initially doubled and then quadrupled, large dairy herds increasingly dominated the landscape. Milk churns placed on a stand at the end of the farm lane became a familiar sight. They were picked up and taken to the station to catch the 'milk train', a term which soon became synonymous with early morning journeys.

As milk was one of the few farm products free from foreign competition it rapidly became vital to the farming economy. The importance of dairying is, however, relatively recent. Before 1850 it represented less than one-tenth of national farm income; by 1989 it accounted for over a fifth.

As herds became bigger, various systems for milking them were devised. The first successful milking machine appeared in 1895. The cows were collected in a yard or shed and then taken through to be milked. One man could milk up to 100 cows in a few hours. However, even as late as 1939, few farmers used machines because they were still unreliable and expensive. Most farms had them by the 1950s, but milking continued to be performed by hand on many smallholdings in the 1970s. Modern milking machines work by means of suction cups placed on the cow's teats and linked to a vacuum pump. A pipeline takes the milk to a bulk tank where it is rapidly cooled and from which it is collected by bulk tanker.

Selective breeding of livestock was undertaken in the eighteenth century by the farmer Robert Bakewell to improve the quality of both cows and sheep. Other successful breeders included the Colling brothers, who produced Durham Shorthorns. Improved breeding, management, hygiene and feeding has been hugely important in increasing the productivity of livestock and has been estimated to account for half the post-war increase in milk yield.

LEFT: St Ives, Cornwall, 1943. With the men away at war, farmers' wives across Britain had to hand milk the cows in addition to the other tasks that they already performed.

BELOW: Milking, 1931. The first successful milking machine appeared in 1895 and as herds became bigger, various systems for milking them were devised. Due to their expense, however, machines were still rare until the early 1940s. Most farms moved to mechanised milking during the 1950s.

Many breeds of animal farmed in the past are now rare. Recent years have seen concerted efforts to rectify this situation, driven in part by the search for tastier produce. The Rare Breeds Survival Trust lists over seventy rare breeds, including sheep, cattle, goats, pigs, horses, ponies and poultry, and is doing much to secure their future. These animals have the potential to contribute to greener farming systems as they can digest less nutritious plants, helping to control the growth of gorse, birch and coarse grasses within ecologically sensitive areas such as Sites of Special Scientific Interest (SSSIs). Since they are often smaller than more common breeds they also do less damage to the soil.

The wool industry, once a key contributor to England's prosperity, declined when first cotton and then synthetic fibres replaced wool in the manufacture of cloth. Today wool accounts for only three per cent of world fibre production and sheep are reared almost entirely for their meat. A third of the European Union's production of lamb and mutton is based in Britain, with around twenty-one million breeding ewes. More than forty pure breeds and twelve recognised cross-breeds exist, which have developed within a variety of habitats; the quality of wool varies from coarse to fine, depending on whether the sheep are reared on the hills or in the lowlands. Sheep grazing also plays an important part in the management of the countryside.

Organic farming

Consumers increasingly concerned about the use of chemicals, animal welfare, the environment and food safety are now seeking less intensively farmed produce and buying free-range and organic foods in ever increasing quantities. The rise of the organic farming movement is possibly the biggest single change seen in British agriculture in recent years.

There was an eighty-five per cent increase in demand for organic food between 1999 and 2001. According to the Organic Food and Farming Report, the UK market was worth over £920 million in 2002. It also reveals that there

were 3,865 organic farmers, including around 600 in Wales and 700 in Scotland. The amount of land farmed organically almost doubled between 2001 and 2002.

Organic growers use methods of crop rotation and fertilisation not dissimilar to those employed in the past. These help reduce weeds and disease, while the careful management of natural habitats encourages natural predators that keep down pests. Animals are reared less intensively and given mainly natural feed, with cows and sheep grazing mostly clover or herb-rich grasses.

The Soil Association has standards that cover all aspects of farm management to ensure a sound and sustainable organic farming system and only licensed processors and farm producers are allowed to use the Association's symbol. For farmers seeking to achieve organic status the monitored conversion period is both lengthy and costly, lasting twenty-four months for arable, horticultural and grassland, and thirty-six months for land with perennial crops, such as fruit bushes and fruit trees.

LEFT: Before the railways made it possible to transport milk over long distances it was sold locally, sometimes by a milkman or milkmaid carrying pails suspended from a yoke mounted on their shoulders and later from large tin churns taken round in a cart. Now the milk is stored in a bulk tank from which it is collected by tanker.

BELOW: The Ford, Redmire, Yorkshire, C 1955. Milk churns placed on a stand at the end of the farm lane were once a familiar sight. They were collected and taken to the station to catch a 'milk train' to the nearest town. By the 1950s, milk wagons often collected the milk and took it to a local depot for pasteurisation and bottling.

BELOW: Rare breed cattle near Settle, Lancashire. The push for higher milk and meat yields has resulted in the scarcity of previously common local breeds. Attempts are now being made to rectify this situation, driven in part by the search for tastier produce and animals that have the potential to contribute to greener farming systems.

In addition to healthier food, organic farming also provides a much better environment for wildlife. Hedges are retained rather than uprooted, providing habitat and food, while field margins are wider. As levels of pesticides and weedkillers decline, populations of insects and animals recover. The impetus of this development has resulted in non-organic as well as organic farms creating special 'wildlife corridors' where beetles and birds can thrive.

Challenging times

Over the centuries the farming community has endured something of a roller-coaster ride, having at times been hit by crisis and depression. Recent years have been no different. There has been a steep drop in farm incomes. There have also been notorious and devastating epidemics. Around £280 million was paid in compensation to farmers who destroyed animals following the discovery of BSE (bovine spongiform encephalopathy) in the 1980s. A further £2.7 billion was paid after the recent outbreak of foot-and-mouth, both to farmers whose animals were culled and to other businesses affected.

However, while there have been inevitable casualties, the industry has sought to prove its determination to survive by demonstrating new levels of resourcefulness. It is perhaps a sign of the strength of feeling amongst rural communities that in September 2002 over 400,000 people marched on London for 'Liberty and Livelihood'. Organised by the Countryside Alliance, the march aimed to make Parliament listen to the opinions of country people.

A current issue of concern is genetic modification (GM), a technique designed to introduce characteristics such as resistance to diseases or pests, higher nutritional content and longer shelf-life. In May 1999 the British Medical Association's Board of Science published *The Impact of Genetic Modification on Agriculture, Food and Heath*, in which it stated:

> We cannot at present know whether there are any serious risks to the environment or to human health involved in producing GM crops or consuming GM food products. Adverse effects are likely to be irreversible; once GMOs [genetically modified organisms] are released into the environment they cannot be subject to control.

These issues have remained unresolved in the five years since the report's publication. At the time of writing, the government appears to be determined to introduce GM in the face of widespread scepticism.

109

CHEESE

Cheese-making was introduced to Britain by the Romans over 2,000 years ago and its popularity has endured – 590,000 tons are now sold each year. The first wholesale cheese-makers in Britain were monastic communities, who disseminated their know-how to the local farming communities during the medieval period. The recipe for Wensleydale (from Yorkshire), for example, can be traced back to the Cistercian monks who arrived in England in the twelfth century, establishing monasteries in the remoter parts of the country.

Today about twenty native cheeses are commonly available, with Cheddar the most popular. It is named after Cheddar Gorge in Somerset, where the cheese was traditionally stored in caves while maturing. There are several types, graded according to maturity and intensity of taste. Other popular regional varieties include Caerphilly (Wales) and Cheshire. The 'King' of English cheeses, however, is Stilton – a blue-veined cheese. It originated in Leicestershire but was named after the village of Stilton in Cambridgeshire from which it was despatched to London's connoisseurs via the Great North Road. It now has protected status, which means that it may only be made in Leicestershire, Nottinghamshire or Derbyshire.

Since the 1980s there has been an increase in the number of artisanal cheese makers. New recipes have been introduced and old ones revived. Some makers use milk from rare breeds. There are now over 400 cheeses made from cow, goat, ewe and even buffalo milk. Speciality cheeses include Cornish Yarg, which is made by hand in open round vats and wrapped in nettle leaves after pressing and brining.

ABOVE LEFT: Cutting the curd to make Little Hereford Cheese, Monkland, Herefordshire. Standards of hygiene have improved, but the actual process of making cheese by hand has changed little over time.

ABOVE RIGHT: Clamping Little Hereford Cheeses in the press, Monkland, Herefordshire. The cheese is made traditionally by hand to the original Herefordshire recipe.

BELOW: Sydney Park, Gloucestershire, 1924. Early motor transport allowed farms to develop cheese-making and other aspects of their business since they could deliver to customers further afield.

RIGHT: Grinding blocks of pressed curd to make Double Gloucester cheese in the dairy of Actrees Farm, near Berkeley, Gloucestershire, 1956.

Rural Britain

Diversification, management and conservation

To make money, farmers have increasingly had to seek out new markets for their produce and capitalise on fresh opportunities. One of the key reasons for this was made clear in a study by the National Farmers Union in 2002 which found that farmers typically receive only twenty-six per cent of the value of meat, dairy products and vegetables sold in supermarkets.

As well as selling through farmers' markets some have set up mail-order operations. The Farm Shop & Pick-Your-Own Association was established in 1979 at a time when around 400 farmers were already selling through farm shops or PYO or both. The Farm Retail Association now estimates that there are currently 7,000 farms selling produce direct to the public. While many of these are little more than simple farm gate sales, at least 3,000 run a farm shop.

Diversification has resulted in a wide range of new enterprises. Venison, rabbit and wild boar are now farmed, as well as more exotic products such as ostrich. Grapes, peppers, tomatoes and even coriander are grown more widely, helped on their way by warmer, sunnier weather and a revolution in eating habits which has led to an ever growing demand for unusual and healthier foodstuffs.

The economies of some of Scotland's most remote rural communities have been transformed by aquaculture with a huge quantity of salmon now farmed. Previously a luxury, it has become something of an everyday staple. However, high stocking density has produced its own range of problems, including pollution, chemical contamination and damage to wild salmon stocks.

Diversification has not only occurred in food: many farmers now offer bed and breakfast, clay pigeon shoots and facilities for caravan clubs. Others are finding success in growing crops like mint and lavender for the growing market in essential oils.

Funding and help are available from a number of bodies. The Countryside Stewardship Scheme makes grants available to enhance, restore and recreate landscapes, wildlife habitats and historical features, while also improving opportunities for public access.

Farmers and land managers enter ten-year agreements to manage land in an environmentally beneficial way in return for annual payments. Over 1,000 miles of dry stone walls and 6,000 miles of hedgerow have been restored, while around 8,000 miles of grass margins have been established in intensive arable farming areas. Areas already under stewardship have seen a marked increase in previously declining bird species, including the stone curlew, bittern, lapwing, reed bunting, greenfinch and wagtail.

A new opportunity for rural areas is the production of biomass crops such as miscanthus, a tall grass, the stems of which can be harvested. These can be burned to produce heat and/or electricity or converted to other useful products such as bioethanol, which may be used to fuel cars. These crops are carbon-neutral and therefore, as a substitute for fossil fuels, can help reduce greenhouse gas emissions and increase renewable energy generation.

Environmental concern is becoming a key aspect of many farmers' lives. There are now some 13,000 hectares of wild-flower field margins, designed to provide a habitat for birds, animals and insects. In England and Wales farmers and growers manage some 230,900 farmland ponds, an increase of 12,200 since 1990, encouraging aquatic plants, birds, frogs and fish.

Around 25,000 farmers in England and Wales have entered nearly a million hectares of farmland into 'agri-environment' schemes, which are long-term voluntary agreements to manage and enhance the countryside.

Farmhouses and barns

For centuries the traditional farmhouse and the buildings surrounding it provided the hub around which the rest of the farm operated. Many farms still occupy these buildings, some of which date back to the medieval period. Most were built

when farming prospered in the sixteenth and seventeenth centuries, a period known as the Great Rebuilding. Most were constructed using local materials and in the local vernacular but prosperous farmers sometimes set out to emulate the gentry by building substantial houses in a more grandiose style.

The word 'barn' is derived from the Old English bereærn (barley house). A major feature of farmsteads from medieval times, it was much more than a place of storage since its design and layout was geared to the processes associated with the processing of crops following the harvest.

Opposite each other, on either side of the barn, were large doors through which horse-drawn wagons entered, piled high with sheaves of corn fresh from the fields, leaving by the opposite door after they were unloaded. Once dry, the sheaves

were threshed using a hand flail, usually made of ash, on the area of floor between the doors in order to separate the grain from the straw.

With both sets of doors flung open, the farm hands winnowed the grain by tossing it in the air using a wooden shovel or scoop-shaped basket called a winnowing-fan. The through-draught separated the grain from the dust and chaff. To keep the threshed grain dry and out of the reach of rats and mice it was frequently stored in a granary raised above the ground on staddles, mushroom-shaped stone pillars. Threshing was also done by machines, many of them driven by horses. The machinery was contained in gin-houses built onto the outside of the barn. Horse-gins continued to be used long after they had been superseded by steam.

113

LEFT: Organically grown salad greens, Dorset. Successful diversification has also meant responding to market forces. There was an eighty-five per cent increase in demand for organic food in Britain between 1999 and 2001; farmers are now making efforts to take advantage of the new opportunities.

BELOW: Glasshouses at a nursery in Essex, 1944. The development of glasshouses in the 1880s meant that crops hitherto grown in warmer climates, such as tomatoes, cucumbers and grapes, could be produced, increasing employment in rural areas and helping to boost the local economy.

RIGHT: Horticultural workers picking plants in a large glasshouse in Surrey, c 1935. While farmers tend to produce the main vegetable crops, market gardeners concentrate on more delicate or unusual vegetables. Most produce is still hand-picked today.

Some barns were built to store the community's tithes. This was a tax of one-tenth of annual produce of land or labour levied to support the church and clergy and generally paid in kind. Fine examples of medieval tithe barns can be seen at Bradford on Avon, Great Coxwell and Coggeshall.

The Dutch barn was introduced around 1780 in order to store hay and straw and provide a shelter for livestock. It initially had a single open side; by the late nineteenth century it was open on all sides, consisting of a simple rounded roof supported on wooden or steel uprights.

Barns have continued to provide shelter for animals and equipment; however, many have been converted into attractive homes that are often not only in wonderfully unspoiled rural locations but usually have a spectacular sense of space and scale. The downside is that they are not easy to convert without losing the unique sense of space and history that makes them special in the first place.

Crofting

Crofting in Scotland is a centuries-old way of life that continues today in the Highlands and Islands. Crofters rent or own a small piece of land to rear livestock and grow produce and many are now diversifying into small-scale tourism and other activities. It has played a significant role in minimising population loss in remote areas while preventing grass and heather from becoming overgrown and stifling other plants and fauna.

Horticulture

In the medieval period, vegetables and fruit were mainly grown in the gardens of monasteries, castles and great houses. The pattern for modern horticulture became established in the sixteenth century, with the first commercial apple orchard planted in 1533, at Teynham, in Kent, by Henry VIII's gardener using saplings imported from France. Kent – often referred to as the Garden of England – has a gentle climate and a long history of growing fruit.

Vegetable gardens were established in the Thames Valley and their produce taken to market for sale. Vegetables were largely consumed by urban and rural labourers unable to afford meat and it was not until the eighteenth century that the wealthier classes adopted the French practice of eating vegetables with meat. This created the market for the vegetables we still consume today: beans, peas, carrots, parsnips, cabbages, potatoes, turnips, radishes, lettuces and celery.

For early market gardeners, proximity to their market was vital. As a result, most were located at the edge of towns. This also gave them access to the large quantities of horse manure they depended on. Rail transport, combined with a rapidly growing urban population, led to horticultural expansion.

The development of glass-houses in the 1880s meant that crops hitherto grown in warmer climates, such as tomatoes, cucumbers and grapes, could be grown. The American fash-

ion for eating fruit as a starter gradually infiltrated the British middle classes, while the repeal of sugar duties in 1874 created a market for fruit-based preserves or jam.

From the 1880s vegetables began to be produced mainly on large arable farms in eastern England. As London expanded, the land occupied by market gardens was required for housing so they were forced to move further out. This move continued in the 1920s as produce could now be transported by road rather than by rail. The use of tractors also made it possible to cultivate heavy clays in places like Bedfordshire. The construction of fruit and vegetable canning factories encouraged some market gardeners to relocate.

Horticulture is now one of the most advanced sectors within British agriculture, accounting in 2000 for twelve per cent of its total turnover; a figure which includes plants and flowers as well as fruit and vegetables. While farmers tend to produce the main vegetable crops, market gardeners concentrate on more delicate or unusual vegetables. The industry contributes significantly to rural communities by providing jobs and is also heavily involved in research and development.

The bulk of horticultural exports go to European Union countries, with the Irish Republic, Italy, Spain, France and The Netherlands among the largest customers. Outside the Union, Egypt is the largest importer, followed by Israel.

Hops

Hops were introduced to Britain in the early fifteenth century from northern Europe, where they were used to preserve as well as flavour beer. When brewed with hops, beer no longer required a high alcohol content to prevent spoilage. This meant that less grain was required, resulting in higher profits for the brewer. Hop farms quickly spread throughout Surrey, Hampshire, Hertfordshire, Worcestershire and particularly Kent in order to supply London's burgeoning brewing industry. Kent had the ideal combination of rich soils and woodland – needed to supply fuel for drying the hops. By the mid-nineteenth century around 50,000 commercial breweries were being supplied by over 70,000 acres of hops, spread between England, Wales and Scotland.

Hop picking was for many years a traditional annual event, with great crowds of women and children from east London and Gypsies from the West Midlands journeying to the same hop fields year after year, camping out in the fields and barns. It was a chance to get away from the smoke and grime of the cities while earning some money.

The hops, yellowish when fresh, were picked into a bin and the pickers were paid by the bushel and monitored by a tally man. The cartloads were taken to oast houses within which they were spread on horsehair cloths laid on a slatted drying floor, to be dried by a constant stream of warm air rising from a firebox below. As the hops dried they became gradually darker and the air was infused with their rich aroma.

Maintaining the kiln during the drying period was skilled work since it was essential to keep the fire at the correct level and turn the hops at regular intervals. The throughput of air was controlled by means of the adjustable revolving cowl at

Working the Land

the apex of the conical roof of the oast house. Once dry, the hops were tightly packed into long sacks or 'pockets' suspended through holes in the floor.

At the start of the twentieth century the consolidation of the brewing industry saw a major reduction in the number of breweries and the importation of cheaper hops from abroad. Breweries now number only a few hundred, and many surviving oasthouses have been converted into homes.

117

CIDER

Made from the fermented juice of apples, cider is one of the oldest alcoholic drinks. It was once produced in large quantites on farms. In the eighteenth century it became a tradition to pay part of a farm labourer's wages in cider. At a time when water was often not safe to drink, the allowance per day was three to four pints; this would be increased during haymaking. Labourers were sometimes rated by the amount they consumed, It was said that a two-gallon-a-day man was worth the extra he drank! Some workers in the west of England were paid one-fifth of their wages in cider. The Truck Act of 1887 attempted to put a stop to this by prohibiting the payment of wages in this way.

Traditionally, cider was made in wooden presses. The apples, many of which were bruised, muddy and unwashed, were gathered and then crushed between rollers. The resulting pulp was layered between straw or wrapped in coarse fibre bags and packed into a press between boards to form a 'cheese'. The presser was then screwed down to extract the juice.

Modern cider making still relies on the same basic principles. Nowadays, large-scale production is confined to the areas close to the cider apple orchards of Somerset, Devon and Hereford, where the soil and climate are ideal. Orchards are also being established in some parts of Wales. Recently sales of cider have grown strongly; to meet the new demand, farmers have planted two million trees since 1995.

ABOVE: Woodmancote Farm, Gloucestershire, 1943. Once crushed, the cider was transferred from the presses to barrels and sold direct from the farm or to a brewing company for distribution.

ABOVE RIGHT: Gloucestershire farm, 1953. Before pressing, the fruit was emptied into large troughs to be crushed to a pulp.

BELOW FAR LEFT: Most cider is now made in factories, but a few farmers have diversified into small-scale cider making, or use traditional methods to make use of their windfall or unsaleable fruit.

BELOW LEFT: Sacks of broken apples in a Dorset cider press run with juice.

RIGHT: Llangibby, Monmouthshire, South Wales, 1936. Traditionally, cider was made in wooden presses. The pulped apples were layered between straw or wrapped in coarse fibre bags made up to form a 'cheese', which was then squeezed to extract the apple juice.

LEFT: Colonel Frank Douglas checks the bag with the gamekeeper during the lunch break at a grouse shoot on the Perthshire moors, Scotland, 1955. The role of the gamekeeper was, and is, to look after the game of his employer.

BELOW: Shooting on the Earl of Craven's Coombe Abbey estate in Warwickshire. Shooting was often the preserve of guests at grand country houses and was a great social occasion for the upper classes.

Gamekeeping

For a working population that was frequently hungry, poaching was a way to make ends meet. As a result there were many skirmishes between gamekeepers and poachers; often these passed into rural folk-law, with the poacher seen as the local hero. The role of the gamekeeper was, and is, to look after the game of his employer. In 1911 there were twice as many gamekeepers as there were country policemen and they often took it upon themselves to enforce the law.

While the Victorian poacher was usually desperate for meat to feed his family, his modern equivalent is often involved in supplying black-market pheasant, venison and wild boar to hotels and restaurants. Poachers still work at night, but carry electric torches rather than lanterns and use four-wheel drive vehicles and even quad bikes in order to capture their prey. The illegal sports of hare and deer-coursing with hounds are also practised all over the country. Offenders are very difficult to catch red-handed as they co-ordinate their meetings using mobile phones.

Managing heathland and moorland

From the earliest times trees were cleared away to provide land for arable crops and pasture livestock. Over the years rainwater leached out the nutrients and the soil became impoverished. The resulting lowland heathland formed a characteristic and colourful landscape of heather, gorse, bracken and grasses, along with areas of bog and scrub woodland. With its generally sandy soil, heathland may appear untamed, but it requires active management; it must be cut back, grazed or burnt to keep fresh tree growth at bay. Until quite recent times it was used for grazing animals such as sheep, while bracken was gathered for use as fuel. Today it is an important resource for wildlife.

Equally important are Britain's 4.2 million or so acres of open heather moorland, which accounts for around seventy-five per cent of the world's total. Situated in the north and north-west of the country, moorland, with its usually peaty soil is, like heathland, not a natural wilderness; it was created by mass clearance of trees.

Rotational burning maintains a balance between predatory species such as foxes, crows and stoats, and their prey. Consequently, managed moorland has a wider range of protected bird species. To safeguard these plant, bird and animal habitats, sixty per cent of the moorland in England is designated a Site of Special Scientific Interest.

Moorland serves as an extensive water supply catchment area. It is also working countryside, supporting rural employment and remote communities through farming and grouse shooting. About 620 estates around Britain, with an average area of 6,775 acres, are involved in grouse shooting, providing 1,250 full-time jobs. This is one of the reasons why large areas of heather moorland were saved from afforestation and over-intensive grazing after the Second World War.

Managing forestry and woodland

Forests originally blanketed much of Britain. They were re-
lentlessly cleared and exploited from Neolithic times as they
both provided a valuable resource and occupied land needed
for settlement and agriculture. Much of the wildwood had
already been cleared by the 8th century BC and it is estimated
that woodland cover was around eleven per cent by 100 AD; in
1750 the proportion was virtually unchanged. Wood was utilised for a diverse range of purposes including ship and house-
building, tool making, wagon and cart construction, firewood
and the production of charcoal.

Traditionally, two crops are yielded from woodland: timber
from the tree trunks and wood from the coppice stools. Timber is felled to be converted into planks or beams while the
wood is used for fuel as well as for rods, poles for wattlework
and fencing and items such as walking sticks. In addition,
trees and forests provide a wide range of habitats for plants
and animals.

During the First World War there were concerns about
meeting the demand for timber. Legislation did not, however,
reach the statute book until after the war had ended. The
Forestry Act came into force on 1 September 1919 and the
Forestry Commission was established with responsibility for
woods in England, Scotland, Wales and Ireland. Commis-
sioners were appointed to promote forestry and the production of timber, and make grants to private landowners.

The first Commission trees were planted on 8 December
1919 in Eggesford Forest, Devon. The war had consumed
huge quantities of timber, particularly in constructing the
trenches. There was a desperate need to rebuild and maintain a strategic timber reserve. The Commission's estates
reached 909,000 acres by 1934 and the timber found a ready
market. During the 1950s planting averaged 24,500 acres per
year, much of it large plantations of conifers.

A mechanical revolution took place and the axe and cross-
cut saw, which had long been used by forestry workers, were
replaced by the chainsaw. By the end of the 1960s timber production had reached 1.8 million tonnes; increasingly, forestry

was regarded as a business. The private forestry sector was buoyant too, accounting for forty per cent of total planting.

In the course of the next twenty years priorities began to change, and by the 1990s the Forestry Commission found itself attempting to balance the demands of commercial production, recreation and conservation. Today the key elements of forestry practice are the protection of ancient woodlands, planting native trees, managing wildlife habitats, and enabling public access.

Some county councils have appointed 'woodland officers' whose brief includes the care of footpaths, archaeology and wildlife. 'Wildlife rangers' control the numbers of deer, rabbits and squirrels as well as looking after natural habitats, while 'recreational rangers' monitor public access and enjoyment of woodlands.

Creating new forests

In the very heart of England, across parts of Leicestershire, Derbyshire and Staffordshire, some 200 square miles of forest is being created, blending ancient woodland with new planting to create a multi-purpose forest for the nation on a scale not hitherto seen in Britain. The National Forest Company was given the job of overseeing the creation of the forest in 1995 and year-by-year one of the least wooded parts of the country is being turned into a sustainable forest for the future. Four million trees have already been planted, with plans for a further twenty-six million, creating what is hoped will be a landscape which will be both beautiful in itself and provide habitats for wildlife.

In the past ten years farmers have planted over eighty million trees. Forestry estates include the pasture woodlands of the New Forest, the great conifer forests of upland Wales and the Scottish Borders, the Breckland forests of East Anglia and the ancient Highland pinewoods.

With nearly two billion trees growing in an area of more than 1.3 million hectares – around seventeen per cent of its total land area – Scotland's trees account for almost half the UK's total. Only about ten per cent of its forests are natural. Most have been planted relatively recently and consist mainly of conifers – spruce, pine larch, and fir – that grow fast in Scotland's mild and wet climate.

Woodland crops

Maintaining age-old traditions, woodmen use a variety of simple tools to produce everything from walking sticks to wattle hurdles. They are helped today by a revival in the use of hurdle fencing and the growing market for rustic garden furniture, all of which involve woodland materials gained from coppicing, suckering and pollarding.

With coppicing, the tree is cut down to within just a few inches of the ground so that the stump sends up shoots,

LEFT: Forestry students training at Faskally House near Pitlochry, Perthshire, 1954. A course of thirty-seven students learnt the art of forestry at the newly created school under four resident instructors and from specialists who were called in from time to time.

BELOW: The road to Restormel House, Lostwithiel, Cornwall, 1906. Wood was and still is utilised for a diverse range of purposes including ship and house-building, tool making, wagon and cart construction, firewood and the production of charcoal.

RIGHT: Charcoal burning, Epping, Essex, c 1955. The carefully stacked wood was thatched with any vegetation to hand and finally covered with fine earth. The heap was ignited by dropping burning embers down a central hole.

forming a 'stool' from which the crop is cut. With some types of tree the stump dies after coppicing; the roots (suckers) remain alive to create a crop that can be cut. Where trees cannot be fenced and there is a risk of animals grazing, the tree is cut or pollarded to between six and fifteen feet (about two and five metres) from the ground. This leaves a bolling which sprouts like a coppice stool but out of reach of livestock.

These methods of managing woodland have been employed since ancient times. They make use of the self-renewing power of trees, particularly hazel, ash and willow. The resulting growth can be cut at regular intervals over many years, providing poles, material for fencing and hurdles for enclosing sheep. When a wood is worked properly using a chainsaw, small axe, bark peeler and bill hook, every bit of a tree is used. Hazel might be cut for bean poles, fencing, walking sticks and brooms, while the bark of young oak trees is essential to leather tanning. Beechwood is used for chairmaking with the turned parts made by 'bodgers' who still sometimes work in the woods using foot operated pole-lathes.

Employing the latest fast-growing willow and poplar hybrids, short-rotation coppicing is producing 'biomass' for use as fuel in power stations. The poles are harvested mechanically every three or four years and are then chipped and dried to reduce their water content and burnt using the latest gasification technology, creating a highly efficient source of energy.

Charcoal burning

When burnt, charcoal provides around twice the energy of an equivalent weight of wood. For many years it was important to industries such as glass-making and iron smelting. It is now used in water and other filters, artists' materials and barbecue briquettes.

Charcoal is produced by burning wood while carefully controlling the amount of oxygen. Charcoal burners were once a familiar sight, working in clearings and they lived in camps in the woods, occupying, together with their families, small huts made of turf and sacking over a frame of poles.

Traditionally, the manufacture of charcoal involved tending the kiln day and night. The wood was stacked in such a way as to leave a triangular central hole, with sloping pieces on top. This was then thatched with any vegetation to hand and finally covered with fine earth. The heap was ignited by dropping burning embers down the central hole. Creating and then plugging small holes in the heap regulated the air supply and controlled the burning. At the same time the charcoal burner built a second kiln. When the fire in the first was doused and the charcoal sorted and sifted, the next kiln was lit so that the process was continual. This method changed little until portable metal kilns replaced earth kilns in the late Victorian period. In some areas charcoal is still made in this way and market successfully as a local product.

Part Four **Communications,
Trades and Industry**

With the advances in communications, trade and technology brought about by the Industrial Revolution, Britain became the world's pre-eminent economic power during the nineteenth century. By the end of the First World War the British Empire embraced not only a quarter of the world's population but more than a quarter of the world's land surface.

Unsurprisingly these developments also resonated across Britain itself, their effects felt in every parish. Improvements to the country's principal roads were followed by the construction of the canals and railways. Country people who had for centuries been isolated at the end of a muddy track found they were now part of something much larger than they had previously envisaged. They could travel further afield and see life beyond their hamlet or village. For farmers and others with goods to sell, there were opportunities provided by access to wider, hitherto untapped markets because of the speed and ease with which their produce could be distributed.

Despite all this there was, and still is, a world of difference between rural and urban life. Villages continued, on the whole, to maintain a strong air of self-sufficiency. From the workshops and yards of craftsmen came the sounds and scents of their trades. In Victorian Britain one could call upon the expertise of the local blacksmith, wheelwright, carpenter, mason, well sinker and cobbler.

Cottage industries flourished behind the facades of humble dwellings. Sometimes sitting at the doorway in order to benefit from the daylight, villagers made baskets, lace or gloves. Others sat spinning, weaving or making candles and rush-lights. Given the seasonal nature of agricultural activity, some form of manufacturing work was vital to a great number of workers in order to supplement their income.

The growing flood of mass-produced items meant that many craftsmen and cottagers eventually found themselves unable to compete. It was not until the inter-war period that light industrial jobs, provided by fruit canning and dairy plants and the like, created a substitute for the employment opportunities that had been lost.

Today, while many villagers offer services rather than goods, craftsmen continue to flourish, although their materials may not be local and their customers may be hundreds or even thousands of miles away. A few craftsmen, such as thatchers, still serve the direct needs of the community. Others are professional artist-craftsmen and women, some of them internationally acclaimed, who have set up studios in the countryside. Many make much of their income from visitors, helping to sustain rural tourism and the local economy.

Roads

From the moment the first twig snapped under the foot of a prehistoric hunter-gatherer, the trackways that criss-cross Britain began to be etched on the landscape, eventually connecting one settlement to another. As horse and wheeled

RIGHT: Horton Quarry, near Settle, Lancashire. Highly mechanised quarrying continues to scar the rural landscape but provides jobs and resources.

BELOW: Pass of Leny, Central Scotland, c 1880. Many villages once had small quarries that supplied local stone for building; in the nineteenth century large scale quarrying began to alter the landscape.

traffic increased, these paths became rutted and virtually impassable after bad weather.

The Romans built the first proper roads with good foundations and drainage – some 7,400 miles have been identified – but after the collapse of their empire these fell into disrepair.

The growth of population and traffic in the sixteenth century placed increasing burdens on the roads and, with the Highways Act of 1555, parishes became responsible for the maintenance of all public highways within their boundaries. However, with an ever growing number of carrier services using the roads and the appearance of stage coaches in the 1650s, the problems only became worse.

A breakthrough came with the construction in 1663 of the first turnpike – a road maintained by tolls – at Wadesmill, Hertfordshire. Although it was forty years before the idea started to be widely adopted (the establishment of turnpike trusts initially required individual Acts of Parliament), 1,600 turnpikes were in operation by 1800. Many of the roadside tollhouses still survive; they were often polygonal or semi-circular to provide a good view of the highway and were built to accommodate the gatekeepers who collected the tolls.

Sound, level roads were vital to the development of the stagecoach network after 1750, and 20,000 miles had been improved in England and Wales by 1820. Dashing coachmen and the sound of the guard's horn became familiar to communities across the country. At the peak of the coaching era in the 1830s, around 3,000 stage coaches and 700 mail coaches were travelling Britain's roads. With the coaches working to a timetable, the infrastructure required to support them was immense. It has been calculated that the workforce numbered 30,000, while 150,000 horses were needed. Typically, a team of four horses might pull a coach at around ten miles per hour for an hour at a time; it is no coincidence that old coaching inns can still be found at roughly ten-mile intervals along the main routes.

Maintenance, however, was still primitive, and the faster coaches put great strain on road surfaces. Real improvements came in the 1820s, with the revolution in road-making techniques pioneered by John Metcalf, John Loudon McAdam and Thomas Telford. These involved constructing solid foundations, which were then covered with compacted layers of stones and gravel. A slightly convex surface encouraged water run-off into drainage ditches at the side. The fore-

LEFT: 'Cat and Fiddle', Buxton, Derbyshire, 1914. The years just prior to the First World War saw major advances in car and motorcycle manufacture which provided increased mobility and opportunities for businesses in rural areas. By 1912 around 10,500 cars were being produced a year in Britain.

BELOW: Hathersage, Derbyshire, 1919. For the lucky few who could afford a car in the early years of the twentieth century, motoring on uncrowded roads was a new and pleasurable experience.

LEFT: Honister Pass, Borrow-dale, Cumbria. As early as the 1940s the popularity of the car threatened bus services. While sometimes limited, they still continue in some rural areas.

BELOW: 'Six Bells', Newdigate, Surrey, 1924. Motor buses first arrived in rural areas in the 1920s and allowed people unprecedented free-dom to visit neighbouring towns for work and leisure.

runner of modern road surfaces, tarmacadam (a blend of coal tar and graded stones) was developed in the 1830s, but was not widely used until the early 1900s. Away from the key routes, the standard of roads in rural areas generally remained poor until well into the twentieth century.

The construction and maintenance of roads gave some, albeit poorly paid, employment to country people. Women, children and older men could often be seen laboriously breaking stones into smaller pieces with a hammer, or clearing ditches and obstructions. In later times, camps of

travelling roadmen with their steamrollers and bubbling vats of tar became a common sight.

The development of steam-powered road going vehicles preceded that of railway engines. In 1834 a Mr Hancock started a steam coach service carrying up to fourteen passengers between Paddington and the City of London. The Locomo-tive Act of 1865 restricted the speed of motorised vehicles (at that time agricultural traction engines) to four miles per hour in the country and two miles per hour in towns; it also required them to be led by a man on foot carrying a red flag.

Communications, Trades and Industry

The first British-built car, a Daimler, appeared in 1896. The Motor Car Act of 1903, its name signifying that the age of the car had truly begun, required all vehicles to be registered. It also increased the speed limit to twenty miles per hour. Following the advent of pneumatic tyres, which had a particularly destructive effect on gravel-covered road surfaces, roads began to be surfaced with a layer of Tarmac in 1907. Rural areas only benefited from this innovation much later and it was often not seen until after the Second World War. As a consequence village roads generally remained horribly dusty in the heat of summer and awash with mud throughout the winter.

Car ownership was limited until the 1950s, with many working men and women travelling by bicycle. For those who could afford it, motoring was something of an adventure with mishaps and breakdowns all part of the experience. There was little help available to sort out mechanical problems. In time, cars and lorries became integral to rural life with the result that bypasses were built around many villages both to speed journey times and relieve narrow streets of through traffic. Ownership of cars in rural areas is now higher than the national average.

Buses

The motor buses that first arrived in country areas in the 1920s were frequently little more than lorries fitted out with crude padded seats. Packages would be piled on the roof and the canvas sides rolled down to keep out the rain. On market day, it was not unusual to find an assortment of livestock on board.

Primitive though these buses were, their arrival heralded a new-found freedom for the rural community. They allowed women in outlying villages and hamlets to visit the local market town and young people to enjoy an evening out at a dance or the cinema. By the 1930s buses were comfortable saloons with pneumatic tyres; they brought tourists from the towns and cities, while the whole village would sometimes go on charabanc outings. As early as the 1940s, however, the increasing popularity of the private car meant that services were beginning to deteriorate.

Today, communities have rallied together to provide their own services by running minibuses driven by volunteers which help to ensure that older people in particular have a degree of mobility. There are also school minibuses and, in some areas, a shuttle-bus sponsored by the local supermarket visits surrounding villages and takes people to do their shopping. Other schemes, often funded by special events and donations, include pre-bookable door-to-door dial-a-bus services.

The Royal Mail also plays its part with its Postbuses which, in addition to collecting and delivering the mail, provide a transport lifeline for local people, and give interested visitors an unusual travel experience. There is a network of over 200 routes to rural villages throughout England, Scotland and Wales. Ranging in size from a station wagon to a minibus, the buses cover 4.5 million miles and carry 125,000 passengers a year.

Signs

The Romans were the first to use milestones, some of which remain in their original positions. They did not come into use again until the seventeenth century, when the first one appeared on the Dover road in 1633. Many of these later milestones still exist; they are usually two to three feet high, with an initial letter abbreviation of the nearest market town and the distance from it. Guide posts, in the form of rough granite crosses, were first used in the thirteenth century to mark the path across the wild expanse of Dartmoor. Both were made compulsory for turnpike roads in 1766.

Signposts carrying village names as well as warning signs began to be erected by the Automobile Association in 1906. Within twenty years, fingerposts made of wood or iron became a familiar sight. During the Second World War all signs indicating names or directions were removed in order to hinder the enemy in the event of an invasion.

Horses and donkeys

Animals were once essential for transporting goods. Donkeys were employed as pack animals, carrying panniers laden with wares, often over long distances. They were also used for farm work, drawing carts and even carriages.

Horses of all types were essential to rural life. They operated threshing gins, pulled the plough, drew wagons and towed timber from the forests; they were also employed on the rivers and canals. They were proudly displayed at agricultural shows and ploughing matches, where they were groomed and decked out in ribbons. In village streets, large stone water troughs were provided for their refreshment. In 1920 a government census revealed that there were around 1.4 million draught horses, half of which were working in agriculture.

Lorries, tractors and cars did not finally replace horses until after the Second World War. Horse-riding, traditionally the prerogative of the wealthy, increasingly became a recreation for all classes. It has boomed in recent decades; stables from which horses can be hired for a cross-country hack can be found throughout the country.

Carts and wagons

Both carts (which have two wheels), and wagons (which have four), are of ancient origin, and were essential to every aspect of rural life, be it gathering in the harvest or transporting timber. Carts could be tipped in order to discharge their contents; tradesmen's versions later had springs. Wagons had a forecarriage mounted beneath the body, which swivelled to turn the vehicle.

Wagons from different areas had distinctive patterns that were influenced by the loads they would carry and the type of terrain through which they would travel.

Since, with the passing of many generations, the ruts made by carts traversing the lanes became so deep that they were as permanent as railway tracks, it was necessary to standardise the distance or 'gauge' between the two opposite wheels; one of the more common gauges – four feet eight inches – was adopted by the railways.

Both cart and wagon-making involved the collaboration of a variety of craftsmen. The body was constructed by a carpenter, the wheels by a wheelwright and the iron tyres and other forge work by a blacksmith. The final touches were

LEFT: Cyder House and Lane, Shackleford, Surrey, 1907. With at least 200,000 carriers operating in the 1880s, the carrier's wagon was a familiar sight in rural areas until it was superseded by the motorised van.

BELOW: Cadgwith, Cornwall, 1911. Carts could be tipped in order to discharge their contents; tradesmen's versions later had springs. Lorries, tractors and cars did not finally replace horses until after the Second World War.

RIGHT: Melpash, Dorset, 1907. Both cart and wagon-making involved the collaboration of a variety of craftsmen. The body was constructed by a carpenter, the wheels by a wainright and the iron tyres and other forge work by a blacksmith. Final touches were applied by a painter.

LEFT: Chain ferry, Reedham, River Yare, Norfolk. Even in the age of the motor car, ferries still serve a valuable service by offering a means of avoiding long detours. The Reedham ferry is the only ferry still in operation in the Broads.

Rural Britain applied by a painter, who used a colour scheme peculiar to each county or district.

The carrier's wagon was similar in appearance to the farm wagon but also varied from county to county and had a canvas covering to protect both goods and passengers. At least 200,000 carriers were operating in the 1880s. They continued to serve communities as late as the 1920s, when they were replaced by buses and lorries.

Rivers and canals

Water has long played a critical role in the life of many villages. Streams and rivers powered the mills. Farmers used floodplains, irrigation channels and watermeadows to make the land productive. The rivers, and later the canals, brought people and goods, often from far afield. Where no bridge existed, ferries were commonly used to avoid lengthy detours; the rights to provide these services were a highly valued source of revenue. In some cases, ferrymen used a rope to haul the ferry across the river, either hand-over-hand or by means of a windlass.

Britain's intricate lacework of streams and rivers has been used since ancient times. In the late seventeenth and early eighteenth centuries many rivers were 'improved', with locks built to control the water level and raise and lower boats. By 1750 over 1,000 miles was navigable by barges. The rivers adapted in this way were called navigations; those who worked on them therefore came to be known as navigators, abbreviated to navvies.

The first canal – the Foss Dyke, which runs from Torksey on the Trent to Lincoln – was built by the Romans. Restored in 1782 and 1840, it is still in use. The modern period of canal building began in 1759, when the Duke of Bridgwater obtained an Act of Parliament to build a canal from his coalmines at Worsley to Manchester. The work was supervised by James Brindley, who was subsequently involved in the construction of a network of canals linking the Trent and Mersey. Canal mania was in full swing by 1792 and lasted until 1810.

BELOW: Tyrley Locks Market Drayton, Shropshire, 1911. By 1840, 4,250 miles of canal had been built. Unable to compete with the railways, however, the canal system went into rapid decline after 1845.

RIGHT: Bruce Tunnel, Kennet and Avon Canal, near Marlborough, Wiltshire. Many canals have been given new life and are being restored and re-opened as their value as a recreational resource is realised.

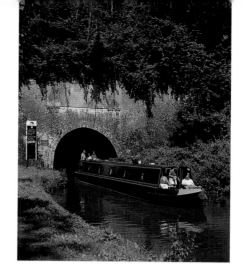

Communications,
Trades and
Industry

LEFT: Dunoon Waterworks, Strathclyde, 1904. Huge engineering projects were undertaken in rural areas to create often spectacular reservoirs and dams that still form the backbone of the water supply network.

RIGHT: Tributary of River Hodder, Lancashire. Rivers constantly erode their banks and today's volunteers follow a long tradition in carrying out reinforcement work.

Canals were both a cause and a consequence of the Industrial Revolution. Manufacturers and mine owners needed fast and efficient ways to move their goods to ports and markets. These needs could not be entirely satisfied by the rivers, and they wanted to avoid using the still inadequate roads. A horse drawing a wagon could draw two tons; walking along a towpath pulling a barge, it was capable of hauling fifty.

The construction of a canal nearby meant the possibility of employment for village men. They joined the huge numbers of navvies who laboured in great teams to create the waterways and, in due course, the railways. These men led a rough nomadic life. Bricklayers, carpenters, sawyers and other craftsmen also found employment, as did quarrymen, brick-makers and boatmen.

The creation of these shimmering ribbons of water, together with their associated locks, cottages, wharves and towpaths, had a profound and an immediate impact. There were additional, and unforeseen, consequences. By enabling building materials to be transported far and wide the canals helped end the tradition of vernacular architecture, which had hitherto been governed by the materials that were available locally.

Life on the 'cut', as the canals were known, was a world of its own. Those who worked the narrow boats took huge pride in everything they did, expertly manoeuvring them through locks and into wharves. They transported everything, from corn and timber to limestone and sheep. Travelling along both canals and rivers, the boats were limited by the size of the locks and bridges to dimensions of less than seventy feet by seven feet two inches. They were usually brightly painted and were pulled by horses, or sometimes mules or donkeys, which walked along the towpath. In later years the animals were replaced by diesel engines.

By 1840, 4,250 miles of canal had been built. A major weakness of the canal system was that the canals' width and depth reflected the dimensions of local boats, resulting in considerable variation in size. This necessitated frequent, and uneconomic, trans-shipment, a contributory factor in their inability to compete with the railways, and the canal system went into rapid decline after 1845.

In the mid-twentieth century most remaining canals were nationalised and taken over by the British Waterways Board (BWB). Many canals have been given new life and are reopening thanks to the work of local canal preservation trusts and partnerships between local and county authorities and the BWB, as their value as a recreational resource is being realised.

Railways

The railways were the pride of Victorian England. Shrouded in steam and excitement, services began in the 1830s. They rapidly made cheap and efficient passenger travel available to all, in the process proving to be a catalyst for huge social change. As the railways gradually reached all corners of the kingdom, people were able to see their country for the first time, becoming aware not only of the beauty of its landscapes but also of the squalor of its industrial towns. The railways had a physical impact as well: stations, viaducts, tunnels, bridges and cuttings designed by the engineers of the day, assisted by the labour of some 100,000 men, dramatically altered the landscape.

The principal roads and canals ceased to be the main arteries of communication. The coaching era came to an end: the inns and tollhouses lost their relevance, with the last tollgate closing in 1895.

Railways provided employment for the country workforce, stimulating agriculture and encouraging the growth of mines, brickworks, limekilns and quarries. Quiet villages were transformed by acquiring stations; some became junctions and railway engineering centres or depots.

Local landowners were often responsible for financing branch lines and it was not unusual for them to flag down the train at their private halt. With the network spreading throughout the nineteenth century, the railways allowed long-distance freight transport, brought mail and newspapers hot

BELOW: The railway station, Silecroft, Lake District, c 1955. Despite increasing use of motor transport, trains were still the prime means for transporting heavy goods from place to place during the 1950s.

BELOW RIGHT: Leamington Spa, Warwickshire, 1892. The railways had a huge physical impact on the landscape as stations, viaducts, tunnels, bridges and cuttings were built by a local force of some 100,000 men.

RIGHT: The mail train, Corsham, Wiltshire, 1906. In their heyday the railways were the fastest means of moving freight. They also brought mail and newspapers hot from the presses in the cities.

from the presses, and eventually gave birth to the commuter as well as the day tripper. People began taking seaside holidays, particularly after the introduction of bank holidays in 1871. Formerly remote coastal villages developed as resorts.

Another important effect of the railways was the synchronisation of time throughout the country. Previously this had not been considered to be of great importance, except for the few people who travelled by mail coach, so it varied from place to place. In 1840 the Great Western Railway led the way, instructing all its stations to synchronise their clocks with London time; other railway companies soon followed suit.

Technological progress also marched alongside the railway in the form of the electric telegraph. Initially used by the

Communications, Trades and Industry

combustion engine. By the end of the Second World War the track and rolling stock were in desperate need of repair. Successive governments were unwilling to spend money on modernisation, leading to a pattern of underinvestment that has dogged the railways ever since. Following his appointment as Chairman of the British Railways Board in 1963, Dr Richard Beeching wielded his famous axe, proposing the closure of almost a third of the network.

Eventually over 2,000 stations were shut and thousands of passenger carriages along with a third of a million freight wagons were scrapped. Much of the rail traffic, particularly freight, was lost to the roads. Following the decision to privatise the system in 1995, Britain's railways are in a critical condition.

One benefit of the closures has been the increase in leisure amenities, with many track beds converted to foot- and cycle-paths. Many former station buildings, and occasionally carriages, have been converted into homes.

Electricity and telephone

The National Grid was set up in 1926, but few rural communities received the full benefits of electricity until much later. It was not until after the Second World War, for example, that farm electrification became widespread.

railway companies to pass messages up and down the line, it quickly became established as a means of sending general information, and the station master began to provide postal telegrams on behalf of the Post Office.

Between 1830 and 1914 the railway network was predominant. However, like the stagecoaches and canals that preceded it, it too was eventually challenged, its nemesis the internal

By the 1960s 250,000 farms had been connected to the grid, eighty-five per cent of the total.

As late as 2003 work was being undertaken to connect mains electricity to an isolated rural community in west Wales where the eleven properties involved were still relying on power from individual diesel-powered generators. This involved constructing nine miles of overhead power

LEFT: Stourton Caundle, Dorset. The red cast-iron telephone kiosk, originally designed by Sir Giles Gilbert Scott, is still a powerful symbol. The introduction of newer style kiosks in rural areas has been fiercely resisted.

Rural Britain line, and erecting over 190 poles and eleven transformers in very hilly and heavily wooded terrain.

The telephone was another service that brought huge benefits to the rural population. At first it was only installed in the homes of wealthier people, with most people relying on public telephone boxes. The first kiosks, made of reinforced concrete, were introduced in 1921. The red cast-iron kiosk, later to become so familiar, was designed by Sir Giles Gilbert Scott. The winning entry in a competition organised by the Post Office, it first appeared on the streets of London in 1926, but was considered too expensive to introduce nationwide. A modified version, the 'Jubilee Kiosk' was introduced in 1936 to commemorate the Silver Jubilee of King George V. Kiosks based on this design were erected in every town and village with a post office: over 8,000 in total.

Mills and milling

Until well into the eighteenth century, wind- and water-mills were the engines of country living and the only sources of mechanical power. They were built to grind corn and pump water both for irrigation and for drainage. As corn (a generic term used to describe all grains, including wheat and barley) was ground to provide flour for bread, the chief staple of the diet, the corn mill performed a vital role in community life, so most parishes had one.

During the medieval period mills were governed by 'milling soke', part of each manor's charter. The mill was the property of the lord of the manor, who therefore had a monopoly over milling. Villagers were required to grind their corn at the lord's mill, paying a toll which usually amounted to one-sixteenth of the flour. Millers, rarely popular figures, were often accused of taking more flour than they were entitled to, and eventually the practice changed so that the miller bought the grain and sold the flour, which meant that mills were enlarged to provide extra storage.

Both wind- and water-mills generally consisted of three storeys. A hoist was used to lift the full sacks of grain to the

BELOW AND RIGHT: Castle Mill, Dorking, Surrey in 1956 and today. Like many redundant mills it has been converted into a private house, probably saving it from falling into ruin.

top floor where it was stored in bins before being released to the middle floor to be ground between millstones driven by a system of gears from the sail or wheel. The resulting flour passed down to the ground floor and was collected in bags. The work of the miller was hard and skilled since he not only had to heave heavy sacks of grain and flour but also had to maintain the mill's mechanism. Millstones wear down, requiring that they be regularly 'dressed', a job usually undertaken in the evenings by candlelight when the mill was less busy.

In the case of windmills, which depended on the vagaries of the weather, the miller had to work whenever the wind blew even if this was during the night. Windmills have been termed landships, for the wooden structure creaked and moved like a great sailing vessel and the miller had to be just as vigilant as any sea captain to ensure the wind did not cause disaster. Fire was the greatest danger and the majority of mills suffered fire damage at some time because the smallest spark or heat from poorly lubricated bearings could easily ignite even quite small quantities of flour when mixed with air.

With the coming of steam power, wind- and water-mills began to close as they could not compete with the mills that began to dominate the flour trade in the 1880s, handling imported grain at the ports.

ABOVE FAR LEFT: Windmill at Cley, Norfolk. Many windmills have been saved from ruin by their conversion into homes and holiday accommodation.

ABOVE LEFT: Wind turbines near Camelford, Cornwall. In recent times the wind has again been harnessed, this time in the quest for a more environmentally friendly means of producing power.

LEFT: Seventeenth century windmill, Acle, Norfolk, c 1929. The open landscape allowed the full force of the wind to reach the sails, but windmills still depended on the vagaries of the weather. This meant that the miller had to work whenever the wind blew – even if this was at night.

WIND POWER

Communications, Trades and Industry

Britain is the windiest country in Europe so it is not surprising that the wind has been harnessed for power for centuries. Introduced from Europe in the late twelfth century, the windmill offered a more efficient method for grinding wheat and corn than animal power. By 1400 thousands of mills, mainly located in the south and east of England, had been established on secular and church estates. Mills were wooden-framed (post mills), or constructed of stone and later brick (smock and tower mills).

Industrial advances in the nineteenth century improved milling technology and windmills began to be used to pump water for irrigation as well as for drainage and land reclamation. By the early years of the twentieth century, however, electricity and steam power had become the energy sources of choice and windmills fell into disuse. By the end of the Second World War, there were fewer than fifty working mills left in Britain.

It took until the early 1990s for the benefits of windpower to be harnessed again. The first wind farm was built in Britain in November 1991 at Delabole, in Cornwall. Most wind farms are in Cornwall, Cumbria, Wales, Yorkshire and Scotland, with the turbines located both on- and offshore to produce clean, and green, electricity.

Wind turbines start operating at wind speeds of around ten miles per hour and reach maximum power output at around thirty-three miles per hour. One well situated wind turbine can produce enough electricity to meet the annual needs of 375 households.

While there are concerns about their visual impact on the countryside, windmills are estimated to have reduced annual emission of carbon dioxide from the burning of fossil fuels by around one million tonnes, while providing sufficient electricity to meet the needs of well over a third of a million households each year.

BELOW: Spinning wool, Portmeirion, Wales, 1933. The inter-war years saw a revival in village crafts, promoted by government schemes such as the Rural Industries Bureau and also by a nostalgic desire to recapture a forgotten past.

RIGHT: Honiton lace worker, Beer, Devon, 1907. From the sixteenth century, lace-making was the primary industry in the Honiton area, until machine-made lace caused the trade's decline. Queen Victoria commissioned lace makers from the area to weave the lace for her wedding dress in 1841 and later to make a christening robe for Edward VII.

Rural Britain

Manufacturing and trades

The image of industry is of a predominantly urban activity. In reality, industry had for centuries never been far removed from rural life. For the inhabitants of many communities it was geological chance that gave them such employment, for they lived above rich seams of coal, lead, iron, tin, and copper, or close to quarries of building stone.

Fast-flowing rivers and streams meant that raw materials could be processed in water-powered mills, while woodland provided fuel with which to make charcoal to heat furnaces. For those labouring in the extractive industries of mining and quarrying, or in the making of gunpowder, the work was hard and often dangerous and many men paid with their lives. The landscape is pockmarked with the tell-tale signs of industrial activity. Irregular hollows, dips and ponds often indicate

where clay was dug, while place-names such as Brick Field or Kiln Lane provide further clues.

Most communities were, to a great extent, self-sufficient. Local people made everything, from boots and baskets to rugs and mats. There were dressmakers and milliners, tailors and needle-women, as well as coopers and brick and tile makers, tanners and potters. The products of each village had distinct regional styles, which reflected the local traditions, materials available and needs of the community.

Cottage industries offered an income for many, but meant long hours and work that was often hard, taking its toll on their health. Generally it had to be combined with working in the fields, child-rearing and housework, and some people worked for agents who supplied the materials and then sold the end-product at a handsome profit for themselves.

Even skilled craftsmen had to turn their hand to whatever was required, be it making simple items or undertaking run-of-the-mill repairs to agricultural machinery. They were generally proud and independent and upheld a jealously guarded tradition of apprenticeship, with skills and tools being passed from one generation to the next. Artisans such as stonemasons often travelled together in bands over wide areas to supplement their income.

Traditionally, villages specialised in certain craft skills. This was often based on local factors; for instance, the production of nets, sail and rope was based in riverside villages and coastal areas. Wetlands produced villagers skilled in straw-plaiting and basket-making. Refugees fleeing religious persecution at various times also brought new skills and products to their new homes. The sixteenth century influx of Flemish Protestants into Bedfordshire and Bucking-hamshire, for example, had a great influence on the local style of lace-making. Frequently, these skills survived into the twentieth century.

Lengths of straw plait, made up in a variety of patterns, often by children, would be sold to other workers who used it to produce bags, baskets, hats and bonnets for sale in the towns. Lace-makers would work by the light of a lamp or candle that shone through a glass globe filled with water and *aqua fortis*, which magnified the light. Needle lace is made with a needle and thread, bobbin lace is made on a hard cushion or pillow with the threads weighted down by bone or wood bobbins.

The demand for knitted, as opposed to woven, woollen fabric, arose in the sixteenth century in response to a major change in male fashion – the wearing of doublet and hose. This required cloth that would not wrinkle when worn. Knitting schools were set up during the reign of Elizabeth I, and by 1600 England was the leading producer of knitted stockings. The mechanical knitting frame was invented in 1589 by William Lee of Calverton, near Nottingham, and was in widespread use by the 1630s. It was not until the introduction, in the later eighteenth century, of frames too wide to fit into an ordinary worker's house that the domestic industry started to decline. However, hand-knitting continued in rural areas. As late as the 1870s, particularly in the north and Midlands, knitting schools were maintained in farmhouses. In Yorkshire, carriers would go round villages in the Dales collecting knitted stockings from the cottagers and delivering a new lot of wool, known as bump, for the next batch. All the family knitted – men, women and children – and it was often done communally, with everyone singing songs to while away the time.

Patterned Fair Isle sweaters, made in the Shetland Islands, have long been prized for their intricate colours and designs. The Shetland knitters continue to develop the motifs and colours of their patterns.

Crafts revival

While the indigenous craftsmen of the countryside moved to the towns for better paid jobs in factories, a new type of middle-class craftsman took their place. The 'artist-craftsman' first emerged with the Arts and Crafts movement in the late nineteenth century. Its leading proponent was William Morris, the reformer, poet and designer. The Movement sought to get away from the frippery and over-designed

objects beloved by Victorians and produce well-made furniture and other items that took their inspiration from the simplicity of traditional skills.

Writers, who saw the continuation of rural skills and customs as essential to cultural life, fanned the romanticised view of country crafts between the wars. In 1921 the government sought to revive rural crafts by creating the Rural Industries Bureau (RIB) which aimed to alleviate unemployment and poverty in the countryside by helping small-scale village enterprises. It encouraged blacksmiths to move upmarket by providing decorative products like wrought-iron gates, weathervanes and lamps. The RIB also found a new market for Welsh textile workers by getting contracts for the mills to produce textiles for modernist 1930s furniture makers, and to make luxury quilts for designers.

The revival in traditional craftwork has continued, generated by demand for luxury handmade items that reflect the traditions and materials of rural Britain. The Internet has proved an ideal way for craftsmen to advertise their wares. They also sell through studios and at craft events and are represented by the Crafts Council.

In addition, there has been a noticeable revival of skills such as dry stone walling, which are required to meet the needs of the strong heritage and conservation movement in architecture and the countryside. As a result, both government and private bodies are running courses and commissioning traditional craftsmen like stonemasons, hedge-layers and hurdle-makers to restore Britain's historic legacy.

Basket making

Basket making is one of the oldest and most widespread craft industries and has changed little since prehistoric times. Baskets are made from the wood of the common osier willow (*Salix viminalis*), which is grown in plantations and coppiced annually. Somerset is one of the main centres, as the flat marshy moors of Sedgemoor providing perfect growing conditions. Willow is also grown in Essex, the Midlands, and Wales.

Numerous types of basket were made for various purposes. There were baskets for potato pickers and fruit pickers, for transporting vegetables to market, and for use in the textile mills. Other kinds of basket included lobster and crab pots, and eel and salmon traps. Trades like laundering had their own particular requirements while a specialised basket was even developed to transport the broccoli crops of Cornwall.

LEFT: The Old School House, Merthyr Mawr, Glamorgan, Wales, c 1955. Thatch is tied into bundles, then pushed into place on the roof beams to create an under-layer and pegged in place with hazel rods. Several layers are used to build up the thickness. A final rein-forcing layer is then added along the ridgeline of the roof, often with a decora-tive pattern.

BELOW: Porlock, Somerset, c 1950. Until the railways made slate widely available, thatch was the predominant roof covering in rural areas. It is usually possible to tell if the roof of an old house was originally thatched, as its pitch will be at least fifty degrees. The steepest pitches tend to be in the eastern counties where sixty degrees is not uncommon.

RIGHT: Stoke-by-Clare, Suffolk. The art of thatching has never died out completely and there are currently some 800 thatchers working in Britain, helping to maintain the 50–60,000 thatched buildings that still exist.

More recently, the revival in handmade goods has opened a luxury market in baskets, for shopping, needlework, picnics, and pets. There are also specialist products such as balloon baskets, conservatory furniture and even coffins.

Willow beds contain about 16,000 plants per acre. Each bed lasts for thirty to fifty years, with the willow rods harvested in the winter months after the frost has taken the leaves off the stalks. A billhook, or more normally today a machine, is used and the willows coppiced by cutting close to the ground.

Green willow cut fresh from the beds is used in living structures. Dried willow is sold either unstripped as 'brown', or stripped as 'buff'. The latter process involves boiling, which results in the tannin in the bark staining the inner wood. Alternatively the willow is cut, kept alive and then stripped later to reveal the white inner wood.

Traditionally, women and children stripped the willow rods one at a time using a shaped metal fork called a brake. In the 1930s a stripping machine was introduced, allowing whole bundles to be stripped by one person.

To make them pliable and prevent them from splitting during weaving, the rods are kept damp; even then, manipulation requires considerable effort. Basket-makers sit on the ground and use a sloping plank called a lap board to support the basket. The maker's tools have little changed since Victorian times and include a bodkin, sharp knife and a beating iron to knock the weave down tightly.

A speciality of the Midlands is 'spale' basket making, where interwoven oak laths are used to make tough oval or round baskets for carrying a range of products, including coke and animal feed. In Sussex 'trug' baskets have been made since the late eighteenth century, consisting of willow boards set in a frame of ash or chestnut.

Communications, Trades and Industry

Thatching

The word thatch comes from the Old English *thæc*, meaning roof covering. Because it is readily available, cheap and effect-ive, thatch is a material that has been used from the earliest times, and was the most common form of roofing until the seventeenth century. It is usually possible to tell if the roof of an old house was once thatched since its pitch will be at least fifty degrees.

In London, the thatching of new houses was banned as early as 1212 because of the risk of fire. However it continued to be generally used in rural areas until the mid-nineteenth century, with a variety of materials employed, including heather, straw, reed, sedge, turf and bracken.

One of the most common thatching materials, until the 1950s, was wheat straw. The previously plentiful supplies were denied to the thatcher by the introduction of the com-bine harvester and new short-stemmed wheat varieties. The most commonly used materials today are long straw (specially selected and managed in the field), combed wheat reed and

155

BELOW: Lake District, Cumbria, 1956. The way dry stone walls are built has changed little over the years and the old techniques are still practiced in the stone regions of the country. In the past the work was often carried out by shepherds to ensure the safety of their flocks.

water reed, each of which gives a different appearance to the finished roof.

It is not only the material that can affect the appearance of a thatched roof; the detailing of the eaves, dormers, ridges and surface decoration also makes a contribution. Regional variations add to the charm of thatch: in the West Country simple, gently pitched roofs with soft curves are common, while in the eastern counties, pitches are steeper – sixty degrees is not uncommon – providing a more angular appearance.

Until the end of the nineteenth century, thatchers not only thatched homes but also farmyard hayricks, in order to protect them from rain. Thatching never died out completely and there are currently some 800 thatchers working in Britain, helping to maintain the 50–60,000 thatched buildings that still exist.

Dry stone walling

Dry stone walls used for the demarcation of boundaries or to form wind breaks have their origins in the Bronze and Iron Ages, although most date from the time of the Enclosures between 1750 and 1850 and are found wherever field, mountain or quarried stone is plentiful.

The techniques for building them have changed little, although their style varies from place to place depending upon the local geology. The waller usually takes the stones from the immediate neighbourhood and uses a hammer to break and shape them. The walls are assembled without mortar and held together by the weight and rough surfaces of the stones.

Large stones are used for the foundations and courses are then built up. The wall is built with two outer faces or 'skins' of large stones and the gap between them filled with a packing of small stones. The 'throughs', large flat stones laid horizontally to bind the outer faces together, are placed about a third of the way up. The wall is topped with a coping of stones; there are many regional variations, including flat, tilted or upright. They are important in weighing down the wall and bonding the inner and outer faces together, as well as protecting it from weather, animals and people. Experienced wallers can build about six or seven yards of wall a day, which involves moving around six tonnes of stone.

Hurdle making

Hurdles are portable wooden frames or screens, mainly used as temporary fences. There are two types: gate hurdles (six to eight feet long and three to four feet high) are made from cleft poles, while wattle hurdles (four to six feet long and three feet high) are made, in a basket-like manner, from interwoven rods. A good maker can produce five hurdles a day. Much work is still done using a billhook and most craftsmen have at least three types: a large heavy one for cutting the hazel or willow, a light broad or curved blade for splitting or cleaving and a light, straight-bladed one for finishing and trimming. Other tools include a hurdle-break or mould, a rail-horse for stacking split rods and a chopping block. The chainsaw is a recent innovation.

Hurdles were once used extensively by farmers and a few estates still employ them for shelter at lambing time. They have a 'twilley hole' left in the weave to enable them to be carried half a dozen at a time on a pole. Today, most farms use aluminium hurdles, so the main markets are garden centres.

Brick making and pottery

Bricks, tiles and pottery were manufactured in the clay-bearing regions, with women and children usually helping the men in the brick fields. In brick making the clay was dug and then left to weather prior to being put into a 'pugging' machine which cut and kneaded it. It was then thrown into wooden moulds from which the 'green' bricks were removed, ready for firing. These were then stacked in clamps and the fuel packed throughout the stack ignited. Since the bricks were fired at different temperatures depending on where they were in the stack, a wide variety of brick colours resulted.

Some farmers ran a pottery business on the side, using wagons to fetch the clay and deliver the pots to market for sale. The pots were made by cottage potters using a foot-driven wheel and then taken to the kiln, where they were fired according to the nature of the clay and its intended finish. Unglazed products were, and still are, given a single 'biscuit' firing, whereas glazed pieces usually have to be fired twice.

The most common form of decoration was, and is, slip, watered-down clay in a variety of colours, applied by dipping or painting. Glazing had been practised since medieval times or before; glazes traditionally contained red and white lead, copper and ground flint. After 1850 a variety of chemical products was used.

The impact of artist-potters like Bernard Leach, who established a studio at St Ives in Cornwall in the 1920s, raised the profile of handmade pottery. Leach was at the forefront of the twentieth century development of artist-craftsmen producing unusual, individual and beautiful work that has become highly collectable. The company he founded is still producing pots.

LEFT: Ewenny Pottery, Bridgend, Mid-Glamorgan, 1937. Founded in 1610, this is the oldest working family pottery in Wales and still continues the tradition of making glazed earthenware for ornamental and domestic use.

BELOW: Carpenters' shop at King Edward's Sanatorium, Midhurst, West Sussex, 1907. Until the age of post-war mass production, local carpenters had to be incredibly versatile. Catering for the needs of the estate or village they produced virtually anything that was required – from windows and furniture to coffins and ladders.

RIGHT: St Neot Pottery, Cornwall. Rural potteries across Britain keep the craft alive today and have helped to raise the profile of handmade pottery.

Carpentry

Converting tree trunks into useable sections involved suspending them over a narrow saw-pit; then a two-man team of sawyers, one positioned in the pit, the other above it, pulled a long saw rhythmically up and down along the length of the timber. The sawyers worked and travelled as a pair. The senior sawyer worked from above; it was his responsibility to direct the cuts according to requirements, which included building, wheelwrighting and coopering.

The joinery workshop often occupied the upper floor of a building, where the lighting was better. Here the carpenter, dressed in a paper hat and white apron, turned the planks, or baulks, of timber into usable items for the villagers, farmers and other tradespeople. The range of items that he produced was vast, encompassing everything from furniture to windows, doors, staircases, travelling chests and ladders. He repaired farm implements and was involved in the construction of timber frames for houses. He also frequently had the melancholy duty of serving as the village coffin maker and undertaker. Carpenters occasionally formed specialist woodworking workshops, where they made items such as scythe handles, rakes and wheelbarrows.

Timber for seasoning was carefully stacked in well-ventilated stores, according to the long-established rule of needing a year for each inch of thickness. Craftsmen often made their own tools and the chest to keep them in as part of their apprenticeship. These were frequently stamped with their names and initials. In some cases several sets of names are evident, since the tools were passed down from generation to generation.

The demand for carpentry skills dwindled in the twentieth century with the advent of mass-produced furniture. Like many other contemporary crafts businesses, the bespoke joinery and carpentry workshops that exist today have often been established within the last twenty-five years in response to the huge growth of interest in traditional houses, period furniture and decoration that began in the 1980s. Some joiners have learned their trade from their father and grandfather, but most will have acquired qualifications at college and are likely to be skilled in working not just in wood but also with materials like glass, stone and metal to meet the needs of modern designs.

Blacksmithing and farriery

The blacksmith's forge was usually to be found at the centre of a community, often beside the village green, and the sound of hammer ringing on anvil was once familiar to villagers across Britain. He not only manufactured essential items such as nails and tools, but repaired farm implements. Dressed in his practical split leather apron, he also worked as a farrier, shoeing the horses of the neighbourhood.

Both an art and a science, farriery is an ancient craft probably first practised in Roman times. Today the trades of blacksmithing and farriery are distinct, with only farriers permitted by law to shoe horses. The Farriers (Registration) Act 1975 defines farriery as 'any work in connection with

Rural Britain

the preparation or treatment of the foot of a horse for the immediate reception of a shoe thereon, the fitting by nailing or otherwise of a shoe to the foot or the finishing off of such work to the foot'. A horse that wears down its hooves quickly becomes lame, so the care and preparation of the foot are just as important as the process of shoeing.

As the population began to drift away from the villages there were fewer apprentices to the craft of farriery and horses were injured because of shoeing by untrained men. In 1889 The Worshipful Company of Farriers sought to arrest this by establishing an organisation 'for the promotion of skilled farriery and the registration of farriers in London and throughout the country'. In 1890 a scheme for the examination and registration of shoeing smiths was brought into operation.

Those who passed were placed on the Register and were allowed to put the letters RSS (Registered Shoeing Smith) after their name. With the outbreak of the First World War the Register served the Royal Horse Artillery well by supplying this, then vital, part of the army with the names of over 4,500 qualified farriers, many of whom were called to serve.

With the coming of motor vehicles and mechanisation on farms, many garages and small engineering firms sprang up on former blacksmiths' premises and county garages built up a steady business repairing farm implements as well as tractors.

The boom in recreational horse-riding means that farriers are once again in demand. Using modern portable equipment, they visit their clients on-site. Other than by training in farriery with the army, the only way to become a farrier today

is to undergo a four-year apprenticeship with an approved training farrier. The modern farrier must not only be able to shoe a horse, he must have a knowledge of diseases which affect the foot and may operate alongside a vet. He may also be asked to tend the feet of cattle, sheep and goats. Horseshoes are now largely machine-made of mild steel, although aluminium alloys are sometimes used.

Wheelwrights

The work performed by wheelwrights was important and highly skilled, since the large spoked wheels they made were often carrying loads of up to one ton over appallingly rutted and uneven roads.

Seasoned elm, oak, ash and beech were used in the construction of the wheels. The wheelwright fashioned the various elements – spokes, felloes (the inner rim into which the spokes inserted) and hub – with planes and spokeshaves before assembling the wheels with great care. The completed wheel was clamped to the tyring platform, a circular metal plate fixed to the ground. The iron tyre was fashioned into a hoop over a fire and then, while still hot, carefully levered into place on the rim with tyring irons. The wheel was then doused in water so that the tyre would contract and, in so doing, tighten the various components.

Some wheelwrights were also wainwrights, making farm carts and wagons, although the making of coaches was reserved for specialist coach builders. The entire wagon was constructed without the use of glue so that the various component parts could easily be replaced or repaired. As the demand for wagons declined, wheel- and wainwrights turned to building and converting other vehicles for rural use and some worked as general carpenters. Before the days of the mass-produced car some carriage builders built the wooden-framed coachwork for motor vehicles, while others adapted to working at panel beating or repainting the sides of motorised vans or buses.

Saddle making

The traditional saddle, with its wooden framework or 'tree', padding and covering of leather, has a dual purpose – providing a seat for the rider and a cushion for the horse. If properly fitted, it will contribute to the performance of both, while a badly fitting saddle can inhibit the horse's natural movement and cause severe discomfort. It remains an essentially hand-crafted item; leather, wood and metal are the constituent materials, while wool, felt, serge, canvas, jute, tacks, nails, thread, wax and glue all play their part along with an ever increasing range of plastics. There are also the accessories – the girth, stirrup leathers and irons.

At one time the tree was carved by hand from beech wood and, although relatively strong, it was heavy. A major development was the introduction in the 1920s of the 'spring tree', This was two strips of sprung steel laid from front to back, which give a resilience to the seat that increased the comfort for both horse and rider. Closer contact with the

horse is also obtained, thus allowing for greater control through the rider's seat bones.

The modern tree is still made from beech although thin strips of the wood are used, laminated in moulds, with urea-formaldehyde resin. Such trees are true in shape and are also much lighter and stronger, with reinforcement of either steel or Duralumin, a light but strong metal alloy.

Attached to the tree, webbing is used to establish seat depth and works with the tree to provide elasticity. Padding is then applied to build the seat. Wool is still used for this although considerable expertise is required. The process of making a saddle is time-consuming, taking some one and a half hours to set a seat using traditional materials, compared with ten minutes for the fitting and sculpting of the synthetic materials more common today.

Apart from the tree, the principal constituent material in saddle manufacture is leather. Traditionally, pigskin was used for making the saddle seat, but it is expensive and difficult to match, so cow and oxhide are much more usual.

LEFT: Church Street, Moretonhampstead, Devon, 1906. With the coming of motor transport the days of wheel- and wainwrights were numbered and some turned to building and converting other vehicles for rural use while others worked as general carpenters.

BELOW AND RIGHT: Saddlers Row, Petworth, West Sussex in 1906 and today. Trades that once played a key role in rural life, but are no longer practiced in many villages, are preserved in the names of streets and buildings.

Part Five
The Community

Victorian villagers, like their forebears, rarely travelled further than five or ten miles from their birthplace. Most were related to each other, if only distantly; they knew everyone, and they knew their business too. Society was strictly hierarchical. Son followed father in working on the land or at a trade, and the landed estates passed from eldest son to eldest son.

While this remained largely true of rural society for most of the century, improvements in transportation and in communication contributed to the broadening of people's physical and mental horizons. Regional styles became less distinct as clothes, farming methods, foods and traditions were exported from place to place. Even variations in dialect and language began to fade following the introduction of compulsory education. At the same time, many centuries-old customs gradually lost their potency as workers migrated to the towns or emigrated.

The movement was two-way. While people living in rural areas sought work in the towns and cities, those in the growing conurbations came increasingly to see the countryside as their playground and as a source of respite from urban life. Many country and coastal railway stations came alive with day-trippers eager to enjoy their new found leisure time, particularly following the introduction of bank holidays in 1871. Visitors also came via the steadily improving roads – there were cyclists, groups on omnibuses, motorcyclists with passengers in their sidecars and, by the 1930s, numerous motorists seeking a pleasurable day out. After all, a picnic on a hillside overlooking rolling countryside was the perfect antidote to the drabness of everyday life.

These visitors, staying for a day or two, would often have been oblivious to the community spirit that existed within every village and hamlet. This spirit is still very much alive. In the nineteenth century, it was the product of a common interest in agriculture; today, the people that make up the community have a diverse range of backgrounds and concerns. Lawyers, IT consultants, writers and tradespeople now live side-by-side. They generally know each others' names, participate in sports such as cricket or football, or join together to fight for their community, campaigning to save the school from closure or to restore the church tower.

Many 'townies' yearn for the quieter pace and friendliness of rural Britain. The fact that they are now choosing to return, even if only for the weekend, shows that there is a continuing faith in the perceived values of country and village life.

The people

There has always been and still is a high degree of stoicism amongst true country people. Life can be hard but 'one just has to get on with it' is a common attitude; if that means getting

PREVIOUS PAGES: Ashbourne, Derbyshire, 1961. Thrown upon their own resources villagers have always known how to enjoy themselves. On Shrove Tuesday in Ashbourne it is traditional to play a football game where Henmore Brook makes up part of the pitch.

BELOW LEFT: The Inner Courtyard, The Biggin, Hitchin, Hertfordshire, 1903. Private benefaction and church funds were traditionally the only means of support for the rural poor. Converted to alms-houses in the seventeenth century at the bequest of its former owner, this building was still housing the needy in the 1960s.

BELOW: St Cleer Village, Liskeard, Cornwall, 1890. As people moved to the towns, the population of this former mining parish fell from 3,931 in 1861 to 2,124 in 1890, when this photograph was taken. Just ten years later, in 1900, only 1,652 remained.

BELOW: Cottages, Hope
Cove, Devon, 1890. Many
village cottages look
quaint, but inside were
overcrowded and often
dark. Once chores were
done there was little time
or space for relaxation.

BELOW: Downderry, Cornwall, 1894. Until the development of the village shop, villagers were largely self-reliant, although some goods such milk were delivered to the door.

Until comparatively recently, life within isolated rural homes and farms was often made more difficult by the lack of running water, gas or electricity. The rural idyll – a neat cottage interior with whitewashed walls and scrubbed floors, where a kettle boils on a blazing hearth and the table groans with food – was largely a myth.

Most cottages were overcrowded and sparsely furnished. Until late in the nineteenth century bread was generally baked at home and it was this, cheese, swedes and turnips, which were the staples, with meat an occasional luxury. Many families kept a pig; when slaughtered, it supplied lard and meat. Killing the pig was a major event, invariably left to the travelling pig-sticker.

The toil was never ending. Cereals, fruit and vegetables were grown and harvested, livestock reared and killed; this was followed by skinning, preserving and cooking. While farmhouses and bigger homes usually had a place to prepare food, including a scullery with a copper to provide hot water, the average cottage offered no such luxury and food preparation went on alongside family life in a single downstairs room serving as kitchen, dining room and parlour.

With the development of the village shop, which by the beginning of the twentieth century was stocking a vast range of goods, including tinned products, the need for self-reliance grew less.

The upper echelons of village society, which included the gentry and wealthier farmers, the clergy, craftsmen, tradesmen and teachers, saw it as their duty to serve the community and care for those less fortunate than themselves. It was these men who undertook to provide government at local level through the Vestry. Named after the church vestry in which it originally met, this body appointed the guardians and overseers of the poor, rates assessors, highway surveyors, parish constables, doctors and schoolmasters. In addition, the

up before daybreak on a cold winter's day so be it. Farming, particularly where livestock is concerned, remains a seven-days-a-week, 365-days-a-year job whatever the weather, often involving the whole family.

The Victorian tenant farmer's wife played a key role in keeping the farm running. As well as cooking, cleaning, doing the laundry and bringing up the children – of which there were many, as families were large and pregnancies frequent – she would work in the dairy, lug food out to the cattle in the fields, look after the chickens and pigs and help at lambing time. By the time the chores were done there was little time for anyone to relax, and money to spend on leisure was scarce.

BELOW: Lower Town, Malborough, Devon, 1927. From 1900 access to secondary education was improved, but in poor rural areas many children were still sent out to work from an early age. Children also helped with seasonal tasks such as harvesting.

RIGHT: Washing Day, Shottery, Warwickshire, c 1890. The lack of running water, gas or electricity made daily chores time consuming and labour intensive. Tasks performed together, however, did encourage a greater sense of community.

LEFT AND BELOW: The Wishing Well, Upwey, Dorset, today and in 1923. The well was watched over by elderly ladies who, in return for money, offered a glass of the water predicting that, if you drank, your wish would come true.

Vestry distributed food and clothes to the poor, ran pounds for stray animals and maintained the roads.

It was not until 1894 that elected parish councils were established. In rural areas, these remain a social unit of real vitality, performing an important role in promoting the conservation and development of the village.

Children

In the nineteenth century, life in the fields and woods offered the more fortunate an idyllic childhood, filled with adventure. They explored their surroundings, gathering frogspawn from pools, collecting birds' eggs from the hedgerows or trees and netting sticklebacks in the streams. They made their own entertainment, playing hopscotch and leapfrog. For the children of agricultural labourers, however, rural life was one of genuine hardship.

Families were large and generally had not only to share bedrooms, but beds as well. While a child stood a better chance of survival in the country than in the towns, the generally insanitary conditions of the time meant that disease could spread uncontrolled. Whooping cough, diphtheria and scarlet fever, amongst others, were common conditions. Victorian parents, both rich and poor, almost invariably lost at least one child to disease.

Children, even when quite young, would be expected to work, spending hours in the fields doing repetitive jobs like scaring away wild birds, clearing stones, weeding, cleaning lifted potatoes or helping around harvest time. The restrictions imposed by legislation were mostly ignored. Girls would frequently be left to look after their younger siblings, do household chores and prepare food. Both boys and girls gathered firewood and, to supplement the family's diet, scoured the hedgerows for

blackberries and other fruits. While boys would generally end up working on the land or in one of the various trades, girls frequently went into service. The 1881 census figures show that there were 1,269,000 female indoor servants.

The contrast between their lives and those of today's children, both rural and urban, is remarkable. Not only is there the freedom from disease, there is affluence: computer games, mobile phones, sweets and soft drinks. The freedom they have is, however, circumscribed, with pressures and expectations. In the past they swam in rivers and roamed the countryside unsupervised for whole days at a time. Today, it would be regarded as neglect to let young children wander around on their own. The generation born in the late 1940s and 1950s thought it quite normal to walk several miles to school and back through all weathers; children are now driven distances of less than half a mile.

The Community

BELOW: Gomshall, Surrey, 1904. Simple pleasures: the modern child experiences a life that could not even have been dreamed of in Victorian times.

RIGHT: RSPB Leighton Moss, Nature Reserve. While children are less in tune with nature than they once were, they have a broader range of experiences, in this case birdwatching at the largest remaining reed-bed in north-west England.

While country children are less in tune with nature than they once were, they have a wider range of experiences. Many travel and are influenced by things far outside their local area. Indeed, the village that they are growing up in is now part of a global village that offers experiences that could not even have been dreamed of in Victorian times.

The older generation

It is estimated that the proportion of the English population aged over sixty was around six per cent in the nineteenth century, when high birth rates raised the percentage of the very young. Then from the late nineteenth century through to the late twentieth, as birth rates dropped and death rates in childhood, youth and middle age fell, came the gradual increase in the proportion of the population living past sixty: six per cent in 1911, fourteen per cent in 1951, eighteen per cent in 1991.

The 2001 census revealed that, for the first time, people aged sixty and over formed a larger part of the population, around twenty per cent, than children under sixteen. Now that people live so much longer and are far healthier, many are, financial circumstances permitting, enjoying unprecedented retirements in which to go travelling and learn new skills.

In rural communities it is often the retired population that keeps the community spirit alive, as they have more time to arrange social activities for everyone and are often key figures within parish councils. They organise coffee mornings, are often the mainstays of the church and, if they have lived in the village long, will know many of their neighbours.

Gypsies and travellers

The first records that we have of Gypsies date from the beginning of the sixteenth century. They were known as Gypcians or Gipsons, since it was believed that they had originated in Egypt, possibly because of their dark skin and exotic clothes. From the time of their arrival in England, they suffered from persecution by the government and sometimes by local people as well. In the villages they were greeted with a mixture of welcome and mistrust; while some envied the apparent freedom of their lifestyle, others saw them as a nuisance.

Generally courteous, helpful and hugely knowledgeable of the countryside, they became a familiar part of rural life and could be seen travelling the lanes in their brightly painted horse-drawn caravans. They would arrive at cottage doors with besom brooms and clothes pegs to sell, as well as sprigs of heather, and would also earn money repairing pots and pans.

There are a number of culturally distinct groups among the Traveller population in Britain: the Romany (English, Welsh or Scottish Gypsies), Irish Travellers, and New Travellers. The Romany are believed to have migrated from northern India in the ninth century, and their language has close linguistic connections to Punjabi. Irish Travellers are the descendants of Irish immigrants who were either navvies, working on the canals and railways, or refugees from the famine in Ireland. New Travellers are New Age hippies, who started to take to the road in the 1980s.

Gypsies and Irish Travellers have always worked as seasonal agricultural labourers, but increasing mechanisation during the course of the twentieth century led them to a more suburban life as road-workers and scrap dealers. Today there are about 300,000 nomadic people in Britain. Many have returned to the countryside, where they do manual work as well as the traditional, but dwindling, seasonal jobs like hop and fruit picking.

Their caravans are now drawn by cars and vans rather than horses and many of the customs of the past have disappeared. Although local authorities were required to provide sites for them under the 1968 Caravan Sites Act, this was revoked twenty-six years later. The 1994 Criminal Justice and Public Order Act greatly increased the powers of police and local authorities to move on Travellers who camp illegally, making it very hard for them to find temporary camps and, as a consequence, many are giving up the nomadic lifestyle and trying to find permanent homes in the countryside.

RURAL FASHION

Practicality has long been the chief concern when it comes to country clothes. At the turn of the nineteenth century the common attire for a man included stockings, breeches, wide-cut shirt, waistcoat, jacket and hat. In the rural communities of the mid- and southern counties of England, and to a limited extent, Wales, the smock was worn over the clothes, to protect them. It was considered unfashionable for adult wear by the 1850s, and was worn largely by children thereafter. By about 1840, working men were wearing full-length trousers, made of woollen broadcloth and, twenty years later, corduroy.

Country women wore skirts that were often shorter than the general fashion, with their ankles showing, while underclothes were of tough unbleached calico. They covered their heads with a bonnet which shielded their necks from the sun. An apron was donned more or less permanently which, when doing rough jobs like gathering the harvest, was often made of coarse sacking. While bloomers had been invented in 1851, trousers were not generally worn by women until the First World War.

In the family, the woman's role included being tailor, dressmaker and knitter; clothing large families meant constant work repairing and patching. Until Isaac Singer invented the sewing machine in 1851, clothes were made by hand. Children, whose clothes were essentially scaled-down versions of those of their parents, almost invariably wore hand-me-downs that were essentially unisex. In some towns there were second-hand clothes shops, while those in service might receive cast-offs from their employers.

Wealthy women with a pied-à-terre in London would wear the latest styles when staying in their country residence. From the 1860s to the 1890s a padded rear bustle was the prevailing fashion, often with a long train. It was a style hardly condu-cive to country activity, yet genteel Victorian women somehow managed to do the gardening, go ice skating and play tennis in these outfits.

New leisure pursuits created the potential for numerous changes of costume. Box-pleated skirts developed for tennis, shooting and even bicycling. Sailor jackets and hats were all the rage for boating and also did service for archery, croquet and picnicking. Men had an easier time of it when playing sport, since they were able to wear knickerbockers or trousers whether shooting, riding, cycling, skating or playing cricket.

Headgear was always worn when outdoors, a bonnet by definition being tied under the chin. In fact, popular hat styles were inspired by rural ideals, like the 1870s 'shepherdess' hat, with its so-called 'follow-me-lads' streamers.

With the surfaces of rural roads still very poor, and mud and manure in abundance, boots, stout shoes or clogs were worn almost universally in country areas. Rubber boots, first developed in the 1850s, became common following their use by thousands of British soldiers during the First World War. By 1845 they had become popular among men, women and children for wear in wet weather.

ABOVE: Shottery Brook, Shottery, Warwickshire, c 1890. Although country women showed their ankles, with skirts that were often shorter than the general fashion, such outfits were still far from practical when it came to doing the daily chores.

BELOW: Arundel, West Sussex, 1906. The children of the wealthy wore 'mini' versions of their parent's attire.

RIGHT: The Old Archway, St Ives, Cornwall, 1906. In 1846 the Royal Navy began to standardise uniforms for the first time. Mimicking the first official outfit, as worn by the Prince of Wales, the sailor suit soon became a popular style for young boys.

LEFT: Eyam Hall and the stocks on the village green at Eyam in the Peak National Park, Derbyshire. Stocks still stand in many villages, a reminder of harsher times.

BELOW: Stocks in churchyard, Trull, Somerset, 1906. An Act of 1405 required that every community should maintain stocks for the punishment of offenders. They remained in use until the beginning of the nine-teenth century.

Rural Britain

Law and order

The role of the petty or parish constable dates back to medieval times. Drawn from the ranks of farmers and yeomen, it was his responsibility to bring lawbreakers to court and to punish miscreants sometimes with whipping or by administering the ducking-stool. An Act of 1405 required that every community should maintain stocks for the punishment of offenders, who were secured by their ankles; these remained in use until the beginning of the nineteenth century, when the administration of justice became more centralised. The constable was also responsible for maintaining the parish weapons, which were stored in the church, often in the room over the porch.

The Justices of the Peace were drawn from the ranks of the clergy, gentry and other village notables, such as retired army officers. In the eighteenth and early nineteenth centuries, the administration of law and order in villages was under their jurisdiction; their remit included punishing petty crime, licensing alehouses, and regulating fairs and markets as well as weights and measures. The constable was under their supervision. At the Petty Assizes in villages, they tried offences like poaching, assaults, abandonment of spouses and families, bastardy, vagrancy, wilful damage, petty theft and other misdemeanours. Crimes such as murder, aggravated assault, bigamy, and arson were tried in superior courts.

The Country Police Act of 1839 empowered Justices of the Peace to establish a paid constabulary for each county,

but this was not universally acted upon and it was not until 1856 that the formation of a rural police force was made compulsory.

The uniform for nineteenth century rural policeman was a greatcoat with a badge, a baton, a lantern and a rattle to attract attention. Taking his name from Robert Peel, who as Home Secretary set up the Metropolitan Police force in 1829, the village bobby was, within living memory, a familiar figure who rode a bike, knew the locals and gave misbehaving children a quiet but effective warning.

Some villages still have resident police officers, but generally modern policing methods are different. Rural police officers now travel in patrol cars and cover a far wider beat, typically responding to emergency calls within twenty minutes compared to the ten minutes taken by their urban counterparts. Helicopters are particularly important where a force has a large geographical area to cover. The Devon and Cornwall Police Air Support Unit was formed in 1982 and its helicopter is used in tracking criminals, surveillance, locating missing individuals and evacuating people to hospital. It is equipped with thermal imaging cameras, night-vision goggles and an electronic mapping system.

Villagers participate in Neighbourhood and Farm Watch schemes. The British Crime Survey showed a decline in almost all crimes measured by the survey between 1995 and 1999, with the fall in rural areas being proportionally greater than that in non-rural areas.

The Community

meetings and living quarters for the constable. Many looked like typical Victorian houses from the outside. Rural policemen in small parishes often simply rented a village house and hung a cast-iron or wooden sign outside the door with the name of the constabulary.

After the Second World War there was an extensive programme of building police houses and in most villages they were built to a standard design by the local police authority architect. However, many were vacated after 1964 as the police force became more centralised and there were very few left by 1975. This has been coupled to greater use of communications technology and, as a consequence, less public demand for local police stations.

Lock-ups and police houses

In the early nineteenth century, lock-ups – essentially, single-storey brick boxes – were built to hold criminals prior to trial. After the establishment of the county police forces in 1839, many counties either extended them or built police houses. The latter typically had a cell, a room for the Petty Sessional

Medical treatment

When country people became ill, many relied on patent medicines or dubious traditional remedies and herbal cures. Their recourse to the latter was a tradition dating from the time prior to the Dissolution of the Monasteries, when herbs were originally grown by the religious orders and dispensed as medicines.

LEFT AND BELOW: Dartmoor Prison Gate, Princetown, Devon today and in 1890. When viewing the modern scene it is easy to forget the way in which convicts were set to hard labour in the past.

LEFT: First and Last House, Lands End, Cornwall, 1927. Standing at the very South West of England, where the Atlantic meets the land, it was the first building to be built on the site and is still a major tourist attraction.

BELOW: The Warren House Inn, Dartmoor, Devon, 1931. Set in splendid isolation on the Postbridge road, its original clientele of miners have long since ceased to fill the bars. Just as at the time of this photograph, its customers today are still travellers enjoying Dartmoor.

For most conditions professional treatment was at best rudimentary. Surgery, despite the developments in anaesthesia and antisepsis, was still painful and dangerous. Even so, the Victorian village doctor had a high social standing, on a par with the gentry and clergy. The surgery would generally be a room in his house; his wife often worked at his side as a nurse, and he also went out on rounds to visit people in their homes. Charitable doctors would treat the poor without charge.

The concept of more in-depth local treatment was born with the foundation of the first cottage hospital at Cranleigh, Surrey, in 1859, where a modest weekly fee was charged to maintain the small number of beds available. The idea quickly blossomed and, within seven years, sixteen cottage hospitals were functioning, with plans for a further sixty-seven. For rural surgeons and physicians, cottage hospitals offered the advantage of allowing them to keep an eye on their patients and improve their medical skills. For the patients themselves, it meant that family and friends could visit.

After a century of campaigning, the need for free care was finally realised with the foundation of the National Health Service (NHS) in 1948.

In recent years, many local hospitals have closed as a result of the increased centralisation of services, but this is now changing. Advances in technology and changes to the way NHS staff work mean there is now a role for community hospitals and they can be developed to provide different levels of medical and surgical care. Telemedicine links are being developed to keep doctors in touch with colleagues at larger hospitals.

Frequently, general practitioners have amalgamated their practices and group practices have become the norm. While they cover wider geographical areas, the range of treatments available is far superior to that which existed even twenty years ago. Meeting the needs of rural populations is not easy, particularly in sparsely inhabited areas. In a pilot scheme in North Yorkshire, villagers who call for an ambulance may find their local doctor turning up on the doorstep instead if they are closer to the incident than an ambulance. Local doctors cover the shifts using a four-wheel-drive vehicle fitted out with the same equipment as an ambulance, treating patients at the scene until an emergency crew arrives to take them to hospital.

Tourism

Improved transportation meant that people from all walks of life could visit the countryside, enjoying it on equal terms, irrespective of class or education. Ironically, in their search for rest, recreation, fresh air and beauty, they often visited the very landscapes that their forebears had only recently escaped in search of jobs and higher wages.

For many residents of the towns and cities, the first sight of the countryside was through the windows of a railway carriage. Others took to bicycles. The Cyclists' Touring Club

BELOW: A visit to the Glen, Fairlight, East Sussex, 1890. New legislation in the late nineteenth century encouraged the building of railway lines to previously unserved rural areas. Bringing town and country closer together, it fostered a massive increase in tourism in the age before the motor car.

RIGHT: Lakeland hills, Cumbria. The need to strike a balance between agriculture and the preservation of the landscape for future enjoyment has been recognised since 1949, when the government began to legislate to create National Parks in Britain.

Rural Britain

was founded in 1878; it immediately became popular and remains Britain's largest cycling organization. The Youth Hostels Association was formed in 1930 as a joint initiative between rambling, cycling and youth organisations, to meet the burgeoning demand for simple accommodation. Its aim was to help all, 'especially young people of limited means', to a greater knowledge, love and care of the countryside.

Today, tourism is vital to the rural economy and in many areas is far more economically important than agriculture, particularly in the uplands and along the coast. With visitors coming not only from Britain but from all corners of the globe, it is estimated that rural tourism is currently worth £13 billion a year in England alone, generating 380,000 jobs.

Many farmers long ago realised the potential of catering for visitors. Bed and breakfast accommodation is available in a huge variety of converted farm buildings, from oast houses to ancient barns. There are facilities for caravan clubs, trail bikers and four-wheel-drive vehicles. Other farmers are involved in corporate hospitality, including clay pigeon shoots.

Thanks to over 100,000 miles of rights of way, not to mention plentiful commons and areas such as forestry commission estates, visitors can explore the country-side by hiking, climbing, pony trekking, sailing and bicycling. Others learn a craft or skill in quiet country hotels. Eco-tourism is a growth industry, with bird watching proving to be particularly popular.

Another aspect of the British tourist industry is the ever increasing number of people that visit houses and gardens. Aristocrats were already showing middle-class tourists around their homes in the nineteenth century. Today it is often a financial necessity and also a key part of the rural scene, with both owners and volunteers involved in organising ticket collecting, guiding and car parking. On a typical weekend, more people visit historic buildings and monuments than go to football matches. In 2002/2003, over twelve million people visited National Trust properties that charge an entrance fee. Many others visit gardens, which are open under the National Gardens Scheme and are listed within the organisation's famous annual *Yellow Book*; the

yellow notices posted along the roads and byways of England and Wales to announce a garden open are now a familiar part of village life.

The growth of rambling

The Enclosure Acts of the eighteenth and nineteenth centuries shut off much of the landscape to ordinary people. However, growing interest in the countryside meant that there was also a perception of the need to protect the right to walk and enjoy open spaces. As a result, various associations were established to help safeguard ancient footpaths. In 1892, the first federation of groups of ramblers was formed in Glasgow.

Around London various walking clubs sprang up and the Federation of Rambling Clubs was established in 1905. Its chief objectives were to maintain and preserve the rights and privileges of ramblers, and to persuade the railway companies to grant them cheap and concessionary rates. In 1931 the National Council of Ramblers' Federations was established. In 1935 this became the Ramblers' Association which, with

139,000 members across England, Scotland and Wales, is now Britain's biggest organisation working for walkers.

In the 1930s Home Counties hikers in their thousands strode along ancient drove roads, paths and trackways wearing stout shoes, khaki shorts and carrying haversacks stuffed with picnics and lemonade. In northern Britain it was a different story; the landscape was just as stunning but the landowners were determined not to have visitors swarming across it. 'No Trespassing' signs proliferated with gamekeepers and the police quick to act when anyone attempted to defy them.

Over subsequent decades there has been more willingness to compromise. In 2000, the Countryside and Rights of Way Act was passed, codifying the rights of landowners, walkers and other visitors. Walkers now have access to huge areas of open, uncultivated land in England and Wales. In Scotland the Land Reform (Scotland) Act 2003 gave statutory recognition to existing traditional rights of access to most land.

Today, while not always enthusiastic about the public walking over their land, most farmers and landowners recognise the rights of others to enjoy the countryside and will raise a hand or nod their head in acknowledgement as they pass by in a battered Land Rover or astride a quad bike.

LEFT: The Blue Ball Inn, Countisbury, Devon, 1907. After the long pull up Countisbury Hill from Lynmouth, this sixteenth-century coaching inn was a necessary stopping point for travellers. Like many hostelries its name has changed over time and it is now known as The Sandpiper Inn.

BELOW: Above Waterhead, Windermere, Cumbria, 1912. Improved transport-ation meant that people from all walks of life could enjoy the countryside. Ironically, they often visited the very landscapes that their forebears had only recently escaped in search of jobs and higher wages.

FIELD SPORTS

Hunting in one form or another has been part of rural life since time immemorial and has provided food, recreation and income. Over time the quarry has changed; deer and hares were popular in the sixteenth and seventeenth centuries, but were superseded in the eighteenth by the fox. In the past otters and badgers were hunted, but both are now protected.

Field sports have contributed to the shape of the landscape while also ensuring the preservation of important habitats, particularly broadleaf woodlands in fertile arable areas and upland heather moors. Hedgerows and copses provide cover for birds while, in fox-hunting country, the use of barbed wire is restricted as it endangers jumping horses.

Country estates were frequently purchased because they offered good hunting ground and tenants were expected to offer no objection. Land-owners employed gamekeepers to ensure that their assets would be maximised and that others would not benefit from their investment. Both the estate workers and locals from the village found employment in the stables or kennels. Others would be called upon to act as beaters to drive pheasants into the air for the guns and would also be involved on hunt days.

Originally, both hunting and shooting were predominantly the sports of the upper classes. In due course tradesmen, farmers and the professional classes began to participate, with subscription thrown open to anyone who had both the time and the money to take part. This was also the time when women arrived on the hunting field, while others of all backgrounds followed enthusiastically on foot, having usually met at the big house where the stirrup-cup would be handed round before the hunt moved off.

Shooting was often the preserve of guests at grand country houses. The birds – pheasant and partridge in lowland areas, grouse in the uplands – were reared with the aid of coverts, strips of existing woodland held back from the plough, or new purpose-made plantations. The shoot itself was, and is, planned like a military operation, with keepers and armies of beaters deployed to ensure a large bag for their employer and his party.

With country sports attracting both British and overseas sportsmen they are capable of generating a huge income for rural areas. In 2003, the campaigning organisation the Countryside Alliance estimated that total direct expenditure on country sports exceeded £3.8 billion per year.

ABOVE LEFT: Chiltern Valley, Buckinghamshire. Pheasant and grouse shooting has become a corporate as well as an individual sporting activity, generating a large income for rural estates and providing seasonal employment for local people.

BELOW LEFT: The traditional uniform of the hunt is still worn. Only the Master of the hunt, whipper-in and huntsman wear scarlet coats, white cravats and black velvet caps. In the eighteenth and nineteenth centuries followers often wore bowler hats or top hats rather than riding caps.

ABOVE RIGHT: The hunt, Wotton House, Abinger Common, Surrey, c 1965. At the start of the hunt, the Master greets participants at the big house, where the packs of hounds are brought together.

RIGHT: Meet at Hawkcombe Head, Porlock, Somerset, 1907. By the late nineteenth century, organised fox hunting had become a well-established sporting and social tradition, which attracted large numbers of participants well into the twentieth century. In addition to the riders, popular hunts attracted followers on foot, on horseback, or in buggies.

Rural Britain

Conserving the countryside

Countryside organisations proliferated in the late nineteenth and early twentieth centuries as more and more people became concerned about protecting the landscape. The formation of organisations like the National Trust (1895), the Council for the Preservation of Rural England (1926) and the Campaign for the Protection of Rural Wales (1928) helped defend rural Britain against urban encroachments. They also contributed to great swathes of the countryside being saved for the enjoyment of the population as a whole.

The National Parks were created in 1949, along with Areas of Outstanding National Beauty, as a direct result of this movement. Ten parks were quickly established, the first of which was the Peak National Park in 1951. In essence, National Parks are areas identified by the government as being of outstanding beauty, ecological importance or public interest. Within these areas many of the responsibilities of local government – most notably planning permission – are handed over to a park authority. The authority has the specific brief of protecting the environment and local community. Although there is no automatic freedom to roam, landowners are encouraged to allow public access and rights of way are actively maintained.

More recently, National Trails have been established as routes for walking, cycling or horse riding through the finest landscapes in England and Wales as well as in Scotland where they are known as Long Distance Routes. The first, the Pennine Way, was opened in 1965 and in all there are now seventeen, each created by linking existing local footpaths and bridleways and by developing new ones.

Fishing

The creation of angling clubs began in the late nineteenth century, when keen fishermen negotiated together for angling rights to nearby waterways and paid a subscription to belong; this is still the basis of modern angling clubs and associations.

Angling – the term is thought to be derived from 'angle', an early word for hook – is now a huge leisure industry, with some three million devotees. Fishing is said to be the country's biggest participant sport and there are angling holidays as well as competitions. Part of the attraction of fishing is that it is open both to small boys fishing with rudimentary rods in their local stream, and to adults armed with the finest equipment, paying large sums of money to fish in privately-owned stretches of river.

Coarse fishing involves fish, such as roach, perch and pike, which may be caught in rivers, canals, ponds or lakes, with the catch often retained in keep-nets before being released back into the water at the end of the day. The equipment can be improvised: a simple rod, reel and line, together with hooks, weights and floats, and any bait that comes to hand. Game fishing, which involves angling for salmon and trout, requires more skill, including dressing the hooks with a variety of artificial lures to attract the fish, and mastering the art of casting the fly with a special rod.

With the development of materials like fibreglass and nylon, fishing equipment has become lighter and stronger. There are 'closed' seasons for catching freshwater fish, designed to protect spawning species, and anglers are increasingly aware of the importance of conservation and of protecting fishing waters from pollution.

Leisure activities

For those who were not members of the upper or middle classes, leisure time in Victorian Britain was scarce and highly prized. Sunday was often the only day of rest, and it was certainly not for frivolity. Gradually, however, the opportunities for leisure pursuits increased. While at the big house croquet, tennis and archery formed part of the social scene, the villagers, thrown upon their own resources, organised activities such as football, cricket and playing in the local band. There were dances, readings and lectures and, on occasions, performances by travelling entertainers.

BELOW: Fishing, Grassington, Yorkshire, 1926. The first angling clubs were set up in the late nineteenth century, when keen fishermen negotiated together for angling rights to nearby waterways and paid a subscription to belong. This is still the basis of modern angling clubs and associations.

RIGHT: Fisherman, Rutland Water, Leicestershire. With some three million devotees, angling is now a huge leisure industry and fishing is said to be the country's biggest participant sport.

BELOW AND RIGHT: Cookham, Berkshire in 1925 and today. Nearly eighty years apart the two scenes are equally tranquil and clearly demonstrate the pleasures associated with rivers.

BELOW AND RIGHT: East
Molesey Lock, Surrey, in
1896 and today. Waterways
have always been popular
and increasingly provide
opportunities for leisure
activities with locks often
places of bustle and
excitement.

BELOW: Golf Club, Criccieth, Gwynedd, Wales, 1913. The first British golfing championship took place in 1860 in Prestwick, Scotland and by the turn of the century golf was well-established as a rural leisure activity with many new clubs.

RIGHT: Bristol Morris, Bromyard, Herefordshire. Often performing energetically on village greens and outside pubs, there are now over 500 morris teams and 5,000 to 7,500 dancers following various regional styles.

Wealthy local landowners would sometimes build a cricket pavilion for the village and join in the match themselves. The village cricket club became an institution, with many cricket grounds established on picturesque greens. Increasing mobility allowed inter-village matches making them great social occasions.

Football grew to be a national sport for both working men and public schoolboys after the rules were formalised in 1859. The Football Association was founded in 1863 and within five years thirty clubs had joined. Football clubs are still a key feature of village life and sometimes, as in cricket, village clubs play each other and draws and social events are organised to meet the costs of transport and pitch maintenance.

In many larger villages there are now tennis and bowling clubs, while golf is a leisure activity that has made use of many acres of countryside, often ensuring the preservation of land as open space, albeit somewhat manicured. The greatest period of growth in the game was in the 1970s and 1980s when many areas of farmland, particularly near the larger urban conurbations, were given over to greens, fairways and bunkers.

Music and dancing

Until after the Second World War, a great many people (both urban and rural) were, by today's standards, remarkably unselfconscious about singing. Women sang as they worked at their chores, children sang as they played games and men sang and whistled as they laboured. Inability to sing is apparently unusual in a traditional society, where the habit of singing folk songs since early childhood gives everyone the practice needed to be able to sing at least reasonably well.

From the 1870s, bands of amateur players, with their highly polished instruments, became an important feature of public celebrations. They were frequently formed in the villages of the northern collieries, where they would march through the streets after endless weeks of practice.

A high point for Victorian villagers was the setting up of the dancing booth for some special occasion. For the young,

dancing was always to be looked forward to, as it was a way of getting to know members of the opposite sex – particularly when the dance was in another village or town. It was also a chance to dress up, although the working lads still wore their hobnail boots and their clatter reverberated above the music.

Ballroom dancing to live bands became very popular during and after the Second World War and these dances were a good source of revenue for village-hall committees, although they were dependent on the availability of local musicians prepared to play for a nominal fee. From the 1960s on, dancing to bands became less frequent, being superseded by dancing to records played by disc jockeys. In the late 1980s, 'raves' held in farmers' barns, attracting hundreds of townies as well as local village youths, became common. These days, community halls resound to the rhythms of salsa, tango or flamenco, as villagers attend classes catering to the latest dance fashions.

The origins of morris dancing are not wholly clear. The earliest records date from the late fifteenth century; 'morris' is thought to derive from the Spanish word for Moor, moresco, suggesting that the Moors brought the dance from North Africa when they invaded Spain. It continues to be performed in Spain as well as in England.

The tradition went into almost terminal decline in the nineteenth century. It was rescued by Cecil Sharp, a collector of folk songs and dances, who first saw the morris performed in 1899 and toured the country, visiting the few remaining morris teams or 'sides', writing down both the music and the dance. The impetus provided by the revival led to the foundation of the English Folk Dance Society. Much of what is performed today is based on his work.

Often performing energetically on village greens and outside pubs, there are now over 500 teams and 5,000 to 7,500 dancers. They follow various regional styles, three of which predominate: Cotswold, normally danced with handkerchiefs or sticks, North West, danced with clogs, and Border, from the English-Welsh border, normally danced with blackened faces and wearing rag coats.

Rural Britain

VOLUNTARY ASSOCIATIONS AND CHARITY

Friendly societies have existed for centuries – the medieval guilds are an early example. They take subscriptions from their members in order to provide insurance against death, sickness, invalidity and other mishaps. By the nineteenth century, given a major impetus by the Industrial Revolution whose worst social effects they set out to remedy, they were involved in a wide range of activities, including building societies, retail and wholesale co-operatives, savings banks, trade unions, and welfare clubs. Between 1910 and 1947, by which time their membership was around fourteen million, friendly societies administered the state sickness benefit scheme. They went into decline following the advent of the Welfare State in 1948 and today there are around 200 societies. Some have grown into financially sophisticated national organisations, while others operate on a very much smaller scale, organ-ising outings to a nearby shopping centre or to the seaside.

Many other village institutions also survive, such as the Royal British Legion, which was established in 1921, lunch clubs for the elderly, horticul-tural societies, amateur dramatics groups, Young Farmers' Clubs and the Women's Institute.

The ideals of the Women's Institute have remained fundamentally unchanged since its foundation in 1915. Today the National Federation of Women's Institutes, to which individ-ual WIs are affiliated, is the largest voluntary organisation for women in Britain and it exists 'to educate women to enable them to fulfil an effective role in the community, to expand their horizons and to develop

and pass on important skills'. Over three million hours of voluntary work are provided by members every year; their activities include the provision of talking newspapers for the blind, and assisting youngsters with learning disabilities.

Countless rural people, both men and women, do voluntary work. It might involve helping to run playgroups, being part of a driving pool or running the village hall. Fundraising embraces everything from the fete on the green to the vicarage tea party to raise funds for the local church. Such activities, as they have for generations past, draw communities together and help keep traditions alive. Much fundraising was undertaken in villages across Britain so that the Millennium could be commemorated with tree plantings, the creation of playgrounds and the building of village halls.

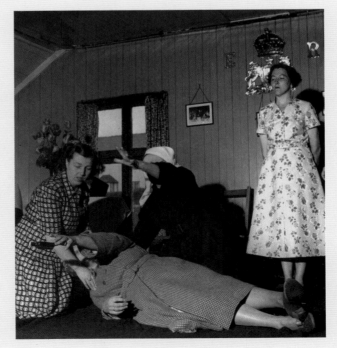

Rural Britain

High days and holidays

Following the Bank Holiday Act of 1871, which allowed six days a year of obligatory leisure, many country people began to enjoy some time out from work, taking day trips – summer outings by train and charabanc were popular – and participating in sports and other activities.

There were traditional parades for May Day and celebrations to mark royal events such as coronations and jubilees. Centred on the village green or main street, these would sometimes be accompanied by fireworks.

There were fetes with stalls, home-made cakes and Punch and Judy shows, as well as carnivals and pageants. Horse- and later tractor-drawn wagons were used as carnival floats, while pageants would often portray the history of the village, with many of the inhabitants dressed up in colourful costumes. All presented opportunities for the people to briefly escape the hard toil of their everyday lives and enjoy themselves.

The year was punctuated by fairs which attracted crowds from miles around. While many had a specific purpose, such as the sale of livestock, they nearly always had some form of entertainment, such as a travelling theatre, or competitions like climbing a greasy pole for the prize of a leg of mutton at the top. Stalls would be set out for the sale of all kinds of merchandise and amusement; there might even be steam-driven fairground rides, coconut shies and fortune tellers.

The hiring or mop fair was often held in anticipation of Candlemas Day, the 2nd of February, when yearly contracts were entered into. Those seeking new employment would carry some symbol of their trade; for example, a shepherd might bring a crook, while maids and other domestic workers would bring a mop, hence mop fair. Such fairs carried on in a few places until the 1920s, by which time many of the old occupations had either changed or disappeared, and few young people were entering domestic service.

The feast day of the patron saint of the parish was an occasion for musical entertainment in the pub or a barn lent by a farmer. Festivities were sometimes organized by the local

LEFT: Hadleigh, Suffolk. Village fund-raising still embraces everything from events such as this summer fete in the deanery gardens to the vicarage tea party to raise funds for the local church.

BELOW: Cotmandene,
Dorking, Surrey, 1906.
In the past dressing up in
your Sunday best on high
days and holidays was
much more important
that it is today.

RIGHT: Wells-next-the-Sea,
Norfolk. There are often
bargains to be had at village
fetes and car boot sales;
but more importantly
such activities attract
visitors, bringing money to
rural communities.

BELOW: Cotmandene,
Dorking, Surrey, 1906.
In the past dressing up in
your Sunday best on high
days and holidays was
much more important
that it is today.

BELOW: Odney Common,
Cookham, Berkshire, 1925.
Going to camp was the
highlight of the holidays for
many young boys and girls
during the inter-war years.

RIGHT: County and agricultural shows, like the Devon
County Show, are still a
highlight of the rural year
and competition can be
fierce when it comes to the
grand parade of livestock.

friendly society. After vast quantities of food and drink had been consumed, there were games and other activities for all. The rowdiness of these occasions was not seen as respectable by the gentry, and this aspect of the celebrations was gradually toned down by the end of the century.

County and agricultural shows are still a highlight of the rural year. As well as being a showcase for new farming equipment and products, there is an element of competition with 'best in show' classes for livestock and stalls of food and other produce that often draw in huge crowds from village and town alike.

Point to points are equally popular and over 200 meetings are held every year, many of which attract huge crowds of spectators ready to put a bet on their favourite horse and rider. All races are ridden by amateurs under the regulations of the Jockey Club.

Customs

Long after the conversion of the Anglo-Saxons to Christianity in the sixth and seventh centuries, pagan traditions remained strong in the countryside, and many ostensibly Christian festivals and celebrations stem from earlier beliefs and superstitions. Rituals often involving the sacrifice of animals were performed to promote the fertility of women and livestock, and the productivity of the soil and the harvest.

Many traditions were absorbed into Christian festivals and feast-days and were celebrated in and around the church. Fountains, springs and wells, which had been revered in pre-Christian times with offerings to ensure a future supply of water, were often re-dedicated to a more acceptable saint. In some villages an annual well-dressing ceremony is still held with flowers and leaves used to create pictures of biblical or other scenes.

In the cider apple growing areas in the west of England wassailing is a custom still performed on Twelfth Night to protect the trees from evil spirits and to ensure they bear a plentiful crop. The word wassail is derived from the Anglo Saxon *wes hal* meaning 'good health' or 'be whole'. The rite involves gathering around an apple tree, singing the wassailing song and pouring cider over the tree's roots to symbolise the carrying forward of the life-force of the tree from one year to the next. It is also the custom to drink the health of the tree, place a piece of cider-soaked toasted bread in the branches to attract good spirits, and fire guns to frighten away evil spirits.

Another custom is that of beating the bounds. This takes place at Rogationtide, the fifth week after Easter, when the congregation asks for God's blessing on the crops. The clergy, accompanied by the church officers and villagers, walk around the parish boundary beating it with willow wands. This had a practical purpose since it was a way for the community to check that boundary markers had not been moved and that no new buildings had been erected. This was particularly important at a time when maps were scarce and inaccurate and few people could read. Until the twentieth century, unruly miscreant children were sometimes thrown into ponds, rolled in briar hedges, or held upside-down and bumped against boundary stones to make them aware of boundaries that should not be crossed.

Many customs are particular to certain counties, and there are frequent variations. Some Gloucestershire villages, for example, still celebrate customs relating to their long-standing cheese industry. Randwick's Cheese-Rolling Day is on the first Sunday in May, when three Double Gloucester cheeses are blessed and rolled anticlockwise around the church to ward off evil spirits. The cheese is then cut up and shared amongst bystanders, a practice that traditionally was meant to protect fertility and ensure future generations of villagers.

In nearby Brockworth a whole cheese is rolled down the hill, with whoever reaches the bottom first claiming it. Not far away at St Briavels, a seven hundred-year-old ceremony involves bread and cheese being thrown from a wall near the old church and then scrambled for – a custom practised inside the church until 1860, when the scramble was thought too undignified for a church building.

200

LEFT: Onley, Buckinghamshire, c 1950. Shrove Tuesday or 'pancake day' signals the beginning of Lent and pancake races are just one of the many customs that continue in rural areas.

BELOW: Kippen, Stirlingshire, Scotland, 1935. Village fairs and sports days always have some form of traditional entertainment though some, such as this duck race, are more unusual than others.

Bibliography

Rural Britain

ARCHER, Fred, *A Country Twelvemonth*, Alan Sutton 1992

BETJEMAN, John, *A Pictorial History of English Architecture*, Penguin 1974

BLACK, E C, *Victorian Culture and Society*, Harper & Row 1973

BRACEY, H E, *English Rural Life*, Routledge 1998

BRUNSKILL, R W, *Illustrated Handbook of Vernacular Architecture*, Faber and Faber 1988

CHAMBERS, James, *The English Country House*, Thames Methuen 1985

CLARKE, Basil and BETJEMAN, John, *English Churches*, Vista Books 1964

CLIFTON-TAYLOR, Alec and IRESON, A S, *English Stone Building*, Gollancz in association with Peter Crawley 1983

CLIFTON-TAYLOR, Alec, *The Pattern of English Buildings*, Faber and Faber, 1987

COOK, Olive, *The English Country House*, Thames & Hudson 1974

CUNNINGTON, P, *Handbook of English Costume in the Nineteenth Century*, London 1959

DELL, Simon, *The Beat on Western Dartmoor*, Forest Publishing 1997

DITCHFIELD, P, *Old Village Life*, Methuen & Co 1974

DITCHFIELD, P, *The Manor Houses of England*, BT Batsford 1994

DYMOND, David, *The Norfolk Landscape*, Hodder & Stoughton 1985

FRIAR, Stephen, *The Batsford Companion to Local History*, BT Batsford 1991

GRIGSON, Geoffrey, *Countryside*, Ebury Press 1982

HOLE, Christina, *English Custom and Usage*, BT Batsford 1941

HOSKINS, W G, *The Making of the English Landscape*, Hodder & Stoughton 1988

HUNT, Roger, *Villages of England*, HarperCollins 1999

JENKINS, Geraint, *The Craft Industries*, Longman 1972

JENKINS, Simon, *England's Thousand Best Churches*, Allen Lane 1999

LANG, George, *English Inns and Roadhouses* 1937

LEWIS, June R, *The Village School*, Hale 1989

LOWERSON, John and MYERSCOUGH, John, *Time to Spare in Victorian England*, Harvester Press 1977

MANSFIELD, Alan and CUNNINGTON, Phillis, *Handbook of English Costume in the Twentieth Century* 1973

MINGAY, G E, *Rural Life in Victorian England*, Heinemann 1977

MITCHELL, R J and LEYS, M D R, *A History of the English People*, Longmans 1961

MUIR, Richard, *The English Village*, Thames & Hudson 1980

NICHOLSON, Graham and FAWCETT, Jane, *The Village in History*, Weidenfeld & Nicolson 1988

PORTER, Valerie, *Yesterday's Countryside*, David & Charles 2002

RACKHAM, Oliver, *The History of the Countryside*, Phoenix 1997

SEYMOUR, John, *The Countryside Explained*, Penguin Books 1979

SMITH, Edwin and HUTTON, Graham, *English Parish Churches*, Thames & Hudson 1976

TREVELYAN, G M, *English Social History*, Longmans 1947

WHITLOCK, Ralph, *The English Farm*, Dent 1983

WILSON, A N, *The Victorians*, Hutchinson 2002

WOOD, Christopher, *Paradise Lost, Paintings of English Country Life and Landscape 1850–1914*, Crescent Books 1993

WOOD, Eric S, *Historical Britain*, Harvill Press 1997

WYMER, Norman, *Village Life*, Harrap 1951

ZIEGLER, Philip, *Britain Then & Now*, Seven Dials 2000

Index

page numbers in *italics*
refer to picture captions

Rural Britain

Photographic Credits

All black and white photographs in this book have been reproduced courtesy of The Francis Frith Collection, and the colour photographs have been reproduced courtesy of Edward Parker, with the exception of the following:

Bryan & Cherry Alexander 118 bottom right, 118 bottom left, Archie Miles 24 top left, 24 bottom, 25, 28 top left, 30 bottom, 32, 33 top, 34, 35 bottom, 36 top, 36 bottom, 37 bottom, 39 top, 51, 110 top left, 110 top right, 175, 193, Aspect Picture Library Ltd. 55 top, /Derek Bayes 150 top left, /Rob Moore 20 right, 20-21 bottom, 23 bottom, /Richard Turpin 79, Collections/Alan Barnes 64 bottom, 141 top, 148 bottom, /John D. Beldom 22, /Oliver Benn 78 top left, /David Bowie 59 bottom, /Dorothy Burrows 140 top, /Asheley Cooper 188 right, /Ashley Cooper 132 top, 174 top, 183, 188 left, /Robert Estall 41, 42 right, 54, 155 top, 197 top, /Ray Farrar 117, /Angela Hampton 42 top left, /Gordon Hill 180 top, 199 top, /Barry Hitchcox 92 bottom, /Roger Hunt 147, /Mike Kipling 19 left, 20 top centre, 66 bottom, /Lawrence Englesberg 198 top, /Andria Massey 56, /David McGill 102 top, /Michael St. Maur Sheil 157 top, /Archie Miles 116 bottom, /Julian Nieman 83, /Graeme Peacock 89, /Robert Pilgrim 123 top, 186 top, /Mike Pooler 73 top, /Brian Schuel 179 top, /Liz Stares 138, /Adam Swaine 71, /Penny Tweedie 113, /Paul Watts 159 top, /Robin Weaver 62, 178 top, /Peter Wilson 102 bottom, Corbis UK Ltd. 96 top, 97 top right, 111, 119 bottom, 120 top left, 120 bottom, 121, 124 top, 165-166, 200, 201, /Richard Klune 26 top, Getty Images 84-85 bottom, 92 top, 93, 96-97 bottom, 98 top, 98 bottom, 99, 106, 107, 110 bottom, 114 bottom, 115, 118 top, 119 top, 194 top, 194 bottom, 195/Roger Hunt 64 top.

Author's Acknowledgements

A huge number of individuals and organisations helped in the writing of this book, so to acknowledge one would risk offending countless others, I therefore offer grateful thanks to all. That said there are three people to whom I must give special mention: Belinda Bamber who spent countless hours researching the background material, Anna Cheifetz at Cassell Illustrated who made it happen and Elizabeth who supported, encouraged and put up with me throughout.